The Story of the
Spanish-American War

BOOKS BY COLONEL RED REEDER

WEST POINT PLEBE
WEST POINT YEARLING
WEST POINT SECOND CLASSMAN
WEST POINT FIRST CLASSMAN
SECOND LIEUTENANT CLINT LANE: WEST POINT TO BERLIN
CLINT LANE IN KOREA
ATTACK AT FORT LOOKOUT
WHISPERING WIND
THE SHERIFF OF HAT CREEK
THE MACKENZIE RAID
THE STORY OF THE CIVIL WAR
THE STORY OF THE FIRST WORLD WAR
THE STORY OF THE MEXICAN WAR
THE STORY OF THE REVOLUTIONARY WAR
THE STORY OF THE SPANISH-AMERICAN WAR
THE STORY OF THE WAR OF 1812
THE STORY OF THE SECOND WORLD WAR, VOLUME I
THE STORY OF THE SECOND WORLD WAR, VOLUME II
SHERIDAN: THE GENERAL WHO WASN'T AFRAID
    TO TAKE A CHANCE
THE NORTHERN GENERALS
THE SOUTHERN GENERALS
ULYSSES S. GRANT
MEDAL OF HONOR HEROES
POINTERS ON ATHLETICS
THREE PITCHERS: ON THE MOUND
BORN AT REVEILLE
ARMY BRAT
DWIGHT DAVID EISENHOWER
OMAR NELSON BRADLEY

With NARDI REEDER CAMPION

THE WEST POINT STORY
BRINGING UP THE BRASS

The Story of the

Spanish-American War

by

COLONEL RED REEDER

HAWTHORN BOOKS, INC.
Publishers / New York

To

DORT DARRAH REEDER

*Dedicated and understanding companion
in tribulation and triumph*

ACKNOWLEDGMENTS

Dort Darrah Reeder, my wife, assisted me tremendously in this story by careful editing and by long hours spent on numerous revisions of the manuscript.

Colonel John H. Voegtly, Medical Corps, U.S. Army, gave me facts about yellow fever. Also contributing information were: Rear Admiral Fred M. Reeder; Colonels Alexander Weyand, John Elting, J. D. Billingsley, and Jack Renfroe; Captain Dale Hruby; and Mr. Gerald Stowe and Mr. Jack Dickinson. Mr. E. J. Krasnoborski made the maps readable. Mr. Carl Pope of Princeton University, Major Morris Herbert of West Point, and J. Metzler of Arlington National Cemetery assisted with facts.

I also appreciate the efficient assistance of Mr. Egon Weiss, Librarian at West Point, and the members of his staff, particularly Mr. William Kerry, Mr. J. Thomas Russell, Mr. John Parker, Miss Nancy Harlow, Miss Charlotte Snyder, Miss Irene Feith, Mrs. Fred J. Moran, Mr. Michael Finkin, Mr. James Pearson, Miss Frances Lum, and Miss Theresa Taborski.

I appreciate, too, receiving from Harold Ober Associates of New York City permission for the use of the brief quote in Chapter 3 from Sherwood Anderson's *Memoirs*. The parts about the firing on the outpost line in Chapter 13 are slightly adapted from *The Little War of Private Post* by Charles Johnson Post. Material about Colonel Roosevelt and his regiment is quoted from *The Rough Riders* by Theodore Roosevelt, published in 1899 by Charles Scribner's Sons.

RED REEDER

West Point, New York.

CONTENTS

CONTENTS

The Story of the
Spanish-American War

1   CONFUSION IN 1898

I N early 1898 stories out of Cuba smoked with excitement.
On President McKinley's desk lay a newspaper with the
headline:

300 CUBAN WOMEN BUTCHERED ! ! !

William McKinley did not read the article. He felt he should
pay little attention to the "yellow press," as sensational American newspapers were called.

McKinley faced a serious problem: *Where did the truth lie?*
For years distressing reports from Cuba told of hunger, disease and death, of a Cuban population oppressed beyond belief.

It was not easy for President McKinley and other cool heads
to evaluate the sensational stories, intensified by scandal-
mongers. For almost two centuries the "black legend" had
persisted. This was the term the Spanish applied to the English
propaganda that pictured the Spanish as cruel and corrupt.

The President was a sympathetic individual, but he resisted as best he could the pressures that urged him to act on behalf of the Cubans. Thousands of Americans wanted him to declare war on "the cruel Spaniards." And thousands more thought him weak because he vacillated. People said it was "America's destiny to move into Cuba, to overthrow the vicious Spanish rulers, and to annex the lovely island."

The New York *Morning Journal,* owned by William Randolph Hearst, was featuring a series of atrocity stories. These pictured the Spaniards as villains, the Cubans as heroes. Then one of Hearst's artists, Frederic Remington, drew a picture of a naked girl being held up and "inspected" by Spanish customs officials. Waves of indignation swept the United States.

The President wanted no fighting. He was definite about that. He had seen all he wanted of war thirty-six years before on the Antietam battlefield, where in less than twenty-four hours the Union lost over twelve thousand men, the Confederates almost fourteen thousand. Late on that bloody day Commissary Sergeant William McKinley organized a carrying party and led two mule-drawn wagons laden with hot coffee, cooked meat and hardtack onto the battlefield. Before he reached the soldiers of his own 23rd Ohio Volunteer Infantry, William McKinley's heartbreaking mission had shown him enough of war.

He was also present as a second lieutenant at Cedar Creek, Virginia, when General Phil Sheridan was hard pressed to win for the Union. In that savage seesaw battle Lieutenant McKinley proved his bravery as a messenger. Now as President he needed a different type of courage if he were to keep the United States away from war.

He hoped for peace, but the younger element in his Republican Party cried for battle. It would take a fiber of steel in a President to keep the United States peaceful. In every state, politicians were vying with each other in denouncing Spain, urging that the United States intervene to assist the Cuban rebels.

Grover Cleveland, the President who had preceded William McKinley, had had the moral courage necessary to maintain peace. When a group of congressmen called and said, "Mr. President, we have decided to declare war on Spain," Cleveland answered, "There will be no war with Spain while I am President... I am commander in chief of the Army and the Navy and I will not mobilize the Army."

Although William McKinley acted calmly and looked like a statesman, people close to him wondered how staunch he would be in the face of the growing emotion over the alleged treatment of the Cubans. He had every sympathy for the Cuban rebels, but he had no firm policy.

Suddenly, on the eighth of February, 1898, Hearst's *Journal* added to the heat on President McKinley by publishing a private letter that degraded him. The slanderous note was written by the tactless Spanish minister to the United States, Señor de Lôme. A spy had stolen it from the Havana post office. Hearst was first to publish the private letter, but soon all other papers picked it up, and Americans everywhere read that the Spanish minister had described the President as a "spineless, cheap politician... a weakling who catered to the rabble...."

De Lôme apologized and resigned, but United States citizens looked on the stupid letter as a national insult.

The President's calmness and stone-faced attitude in the teeth of the crisis irritated many Americans, particularly a political leader in his own Republican Party who had the energy of a dynamo, Theodore Roosevelt. Roosevelt and his friend Dr. Leonard Wood, a former Indian fighter and now physician to the President and his wife, felt war against Spain "would be righteous . . . and in the best interests of the nation. . . ."

When William McKinley hesitated about going to war, Roosevelt told friends that the President "had no more back-bone than a chocolate éclair." Three years later, at the time of McKinley's assassination, Roosevelt softened this harsh criticism by telling Congress that "William McKinley was the most widely loved man in the United States. . . . No one could fail to respect him."

Although the President teased Roosevelt by asking him when he was going to declare war, McKinley liked this virile, tempestuous American. As Assistant Secretary of the Navy, Roosevelt cut red tape and led the way in overhauling the Navy. It was chiefly because of him that the Navy was ready to fight.

There were no gray areas for Theodore Roosevelt; every-thing was either right or wrong. When he was given a job he pursued it as if he had to perform every function. When as head of the New York City police board he saw a police-man drinking, he personally brought him up for punishment. If the policeman ran, he chased him. Roosevelt was a dynamic public speaker; he was at home with cowboys, politicians, and intellectuals, although he disbelieved in many of the latter. A graduate of Harvard and a student at Columbia, he read everything he could get his hands on. One of his most admirable traits was his willingness to speak his mind, "even at the cost of jeopardizing my place," as he wrote his brother-in-law. It made him outstanding.

The speeches of the forty-year-old dynamo were not ap-preciated by his sixty-year-old boss, a former governor of Massachusetts, Secretary of the Navy John D. Long. Long reprimanded Roosevelt once for talking too much, and he promised to be good. In a private letter he expressed his feel-ings by referring to Secretary Long as "a perfect dear."

When reports from Cuba became more frenzied, Roosevelt and thousands of other warlike Americans called for a fight. It seemed un-American to them to stand by when reports described how a Spanish general was slaughtering Cubans. Rioting had broken out in Havana. Americans living there were in danger. The American Consul General, the former Confederate cavalry leader Fitzhugh Lee, nephew of Robert E. Lee, did not scare easily. He reported conditions to Washington, and the battleship U.S.S. *Maine* steamed into Havana Harbor. This was January, 1898.

The slim white warship dropped anchor not far from Morro Castle, Spanish fortress of a bygone day. The *Maine* was on a "courtesy visit," but many citizens of Havana were furious. To them the warship represented the might of the United States, and that is exactly what the President and his advisors had hoped. Perhaps the presence of the *Maine* could deter war.

2   THE YEARS BACK...

THE battleship *Maine*, riding the gentle swells in Havana harbor, was a modern symbol of the world's interest in Cuba.

Cuba had held the attention of people in one way or another ever since Christopher Columbus discovered the beautiful island in 1492. Its history of bloody strife began nineteen years later when Diego Velázquez, one of the Spanish conquerors, gained a foothold, founded several towns, and established a base for Spanish explorations into the Americas.

The treasure fleets of the Spaniards attracted sea wolves to Cuban waters as honey attracts bears. The buccaneers also plundered towns, but in spite of the pirates Cuba prospered. Then Negro slaves were brought in, and the Arawak Indians, who had settled in Cuba from South America, intermarried and died off. A miserable existence incited the Negroes, and they revolted. Turmoil became an integral part of Cuban life, and it has continued to the present day.

At the end of the French and Indian Wars the English

8

realized that if they owned Cuba it would help their American colonies, so the English seized Havana and held there for a year but could not take the island from the Spanish.

After the United States was formed, many Americans wanted the sugar-producing country—not just because of its wealth, but for fear an enemy might use it as a base for an attack against the United States. Thomas Jefferson went even further. He wrote, "[The addition of Cuba] is exactly what is wanted to advance our power as a nation. . . ."

President James Polk, in 1845, tried to buy Cuba for $100 million but the Spanish were opposed. They said they would rather see Cuba "sunk in the ocean."

A few years later impetuous American volunteers, adventurers known as filibusters, organized private, armed expeditions to raid Cuba, Mexico, Central and South American countries. These piratical men thirsted for loot. The strangest of the filibusters was a former colonel of Spanish cavalry, Narciso Lopez, a little man with dangerous characteristics: He was unscrupulous, a poor planner, and possessed a magnetic personality. "General" Lopez, as he called himself, recruited about 250 men in Ohio and Kentucky and assembled them in New Orleans. This pirate assured his followers, "Once we are ashore the Cuban Rebels will flock to my standard."

He led three expeditions of "liberators" to Cuba, but the Cubans avoided them like the plague. Lopez brought death to many, and he met his own end when the Spanish army captured him in Cuba and placed him on a stand with a garrote. An iron collar was fastened about his neck while a crowd of twenty thousand watched. After a priest had administered the last rites the executioner twisted the thumbscrew, and Lopez was strangled.

From 1850 until the war began, scores of troublesome Americans such as "Dynamite Johnny" O'Brien made a business of running arms and ammunition to Central American countries and to Cuba. On one trip he had along young Fred Funston of Kansas, an adventurous leader who would become famous in the Philippine Insurrection.

In New York and Florida Cuban leaders spread propaganda, sold bonds, and plotted rebellion—in Cuba. These Cubans, known as the junta,* worked to advertise the plight of the Cuban people and to stir up hatred against Spain.

In addition, the economic stake of the United States citizens in Cuba was growing, because Americans were attracted by the opportunities of making money through the sugar and mining industries. The United States was becoming involved in Cuba.

During the years before the Civil War in the United States, three American ministers to Europe drew up a scheme that surpassed any dream of the filibusters. The three ministers, meeting at Ostend, Belgium, in 1854, planned to buy all of the island for $120 million. If Spain refused to sell, the plot was for the United States to seize Cuba by force. The document outlining this wild idea was called the Ostend Manifesto.

This plan stirred hatred. In the Northern states it was feared Cuba would come in as a slave state. Northern fears were groundless—once again Spain refused to sell. A crisis was averted when the American Secretary of State repudiated this curious document.

James Buchanan, the weak President just before the Civil War, urged in three State-of-the-Union messages that the United States acquire the island, but with war on the horizon people refused to listen. After the Civil War, President Andrew Johnson predicted that eventually the United States would have to face the issue.

In 1868 the island was boiling. Guerrilla warfare (sporadic fighting without pitched battles) started and lasted a decade.

* Pronounced "hunta." This fraternity, or union, called itself the Cuban government.

It was bloody, close-in combat, with neither side giving quarter. In the Ten Years' War, when a Cuban rebel was discovered or captured, the Spaniards conducted ruthless reprisals against his relatives.

An inspirational young man, one of the best writers of Spanish-America, José Julian Martí, worked for Cuba's liberation in South America and in the United States, where he founded the Cuban Revolutionary Party. The Spaniards had known of Martí since he was sixteen because he published poems and statements that buoyed the rebels, such as,

> Oh, how sweet it is to die when one dies
> Fighting audaciously to defend one's country!

This brought the devoted Martí a six-year prison sentence with a ball and chain riveted to his ankle. Fortunately for him, after one year in jail friends secured his release, and his sentence was commuted to exile in Spain.

Cuba was becoming an island of death. President Grant recognized this when he told Congress, "...For the last seven years there has been raging in Cuba a ruinous conflict.... Desolation... and the torch [are] the agents...." Ulysses S. Grant proposed mediation, but Spain's answer was to pour more and more soldiers into Cuba, until the total reached two hundred thousand. Before the Ten Years' War ended, about that many Cubans and Spaniards had perished.

When the fighting ceased, Spain saddled the cost of the war, almost a billion dollars, on the Cubans. The almost unbelievable situation tightened even more for the Cubans because of an economic depression in the United States. The price of sugar and the demand for tobacco fell just five years before the *Maine* sailed into Havana Harbor.

Rebel leaders who had fled from the Spaniards in the Ten Years' War now began to return to the island. Antonio Maceo, "the Lion"—a huge mulatto, one of the greatest military leaders the Negro race has produced—worked to organize the rebels. Máximo Gómez, a Dominican general and a natural leader, was so emotional he fell to his knees and kissed the soil of Cuba when he landed to lead the rebels. Another Cuban military commander of ability was the Cuban Indian Calixto García Íñiguez.

The situation on the island continued to deteriorate. When the rebel leaders ordered their followers to set sugar mills on fire in 1896, the Spaniards brought in a severe, unmerciful man. This was General Valeriano Weyler y Nicolau.

Governor-General Weyler, able but with ice in his veins, met terror with terror. He was a hard-looking man: wide black moustache, long nose and grim mouth; and his first orders went further than even the rebel leaders had envisioned. He ordered cane fields set on fire and, worse, he said, "*Reconcentrado!*" By this he meant to uproot the rural population of the island and herd men, women and children into concentration camps near towns where they could be watched and where they could give no aid to rebel guerrillas.

It meant death if anyone left one of Weyler's concentration camps. Life in them was stifling. Shortly the reconcentrados discovered an even worse fate: starvation for lack of supplies. Reports said that fifty thousand perished in the province of Havana alone.

Back in Washington, Clara Barton, philanthropist from Oxford, Massachusetts, walked into the President's office. She was famous. As a girl she had become interested in Army people through her father, who served in the Indian Wars under Mad Anthony Wayne. In the Civil War, as a member of the hospital service, Clara Barton helped sick and wounded Union soldiers, and at her own cost organized searches for missing men. She was a prime force in the establishment of the American Red Cross.

Clara Barton was appalled by stories of the starving reconcentrados, and although she was now seventy-seven, she decided to do something about it. With McKinley's permission she sailed for Cuba with a shipload of supplies. When she arrived, thousands flocked to see her because the rumor sped about that she was going to give away money. The appearance of the reconcentrados was frightful. She described them, in her book, *The Red Cross:*

In a large building in Havana [I saw] over four hundred women and children in the most pitiable condition possible for human beings to be in and live. ... The death record counted out a dozen or more every twenty-four hours, and the grim, terrible pile of black coffins that confronted one at the very doorway told each famishing applicant on her entrance what her exit was likely to be. ... Some were mere skeletons, others swollen out of all human shape. ... Massacres [I had recently seen] in Armenia seemed merciful by comparison.

She visited the town of Jaruco, twenty miles from Havana, and found a city of devastation, peopled almost entirely by reconcentrados.

On the Spanish side, the Spaniards complained that the rebel soldiers were destroying gardens intended for the penned-up Cubans. In any event, regardless of the efforts of the American Red Cross and other relief agencies, there was not enough food on the island.

With the Cuban junta spreading news of "Butcher" Weyler and his cruelty and telling only one side of the terror that gripped the island, thousands of Americans felt angry. American trade with Cuba all but stopped again, and American investments on the island became practically worthless.

It was at this time that William Randolph Hearst, of the New York *Morning Journal,* and Joseph Pulitzer, who owned the New York *World,* saw opportunities to increase the circulation of their papers by publishing floods of hair-raising stories out of Cuba. Big headlines developed. To gather news of Butcher Weyler and the revolt, Hearst sent twenty correspondents into Cuba and hired ten dispatch boats to bring back their reports. One of the writers he sent to the island was Richard Harding Davis, a dashing world traveler and the most famous war correspondent of the day. Hearst paid him three thousand dollars per month. War with Spain seemed unavoidable in this excitement and because of the United States' love for the underdog rebels.

Frederic Remington, famous for his drawings and paintings of life on the Western plains, became unhappy working for Hearst. After his drawing of the naked girl being inspected by Spanish officials, Remington told Hearst that he had had enough. A story spread that Hearst tried to entice the artist into staying on the job by saying, "Please remain. You furnish the pictures. I will furnish the war."

In Cuba, to see war firsthand with General Campos' guerrillas, was a young subaltern on brief leave from His Majesty's Hussars, Winston Churchill. There was not much action with Campos at this time, but on a chase after the enemy a few bullets cracked over Churchill, his first time under fire but hardly his last. Churchill saw little excitement with the guerrillas.

To try to keep from war, President McKinley attempted diplomatic action, urging Spain to make reforms on the island. Because the Spanish were not anxious to make war so far from home, they recalled General Weyler; and when the *Maine* anchored in Havana Harbor, Spanish officials were extremely courteous to the naval officers.

Suddenly, on the evening of February 15, 1898, there was a ghastly roar in the harbor. The battleship *Maine* rose partly out of the water, then sank. In a few minutes it had carried 260 officers and men to the bottom.

U.S.S. MAINE

3 NIGHTMARE FOR THE PRESIDENT

AT three o'clock in the morning the telephone tinkled at President McKinley's bedside. The voice startling the sleepy President was that of Secretary Long. "Frightful news! The *Maine* has been blown up! In Havana Harbor."

"What?" gasped the President. "Incredible! Repeat that. How do you know?"

"Captain Sigsbee sent me a cable."

"Who?"

"The captain of the *Maine*. He was not killed."

"How many were? This is dreadful."

Then Long read Sigsbee's message. It gave the horrible details and added that wounded and survivors had been taken aboard a Spanish man-of-war and a Ward Line steamer, and that many Spanish officers had expressed sympathy.

The President was stunned. He asked if the explosion had been an accident, sabotage, or an act of war. Long could not say.

When the news broke, tremendous excitement and indignation swept the nation. People were aghast. They expected war to be declared instantly. Hearst's *Journal* carried a headline in its biggest and boldest type:

MAINE HAS BEEN BLOWN UP! HUNDREDS OF SAILORS KILLED!

There was a great outcry. Many newspapers leaped to the conclusion that the battleship was blown up deliberately by the Spaniards. McKinley aged overnight. Dark circles ringed his eyes.

The Party and Congress would do what McKinley wanted. He felt trapped because he saw it would be necessary to give in to demands for war in order to retain control of the Republican Party. "The country is just not ready for war," he kept repeating to members of his Cabinet. It would have been more accurate if he had said, "Our Army especially is not ready to fight."

On the heels of the cable from Havana came another message, remarkably cool, signed "SIGSBEE:"

PUBLIC OPINION SHOULD BE SUSPENDED
UNTIL FURTHER REPORT.

But the New York *Morning Journal* accepted the assumption that the *Maine* had been sunk deliberately. It announced on its front page:

$50,000 REWARD ! ! !

MR. W. R. HEARST HAS PLACED ON DEPOSIT WITH THE WELLS, FARGO CO. TO BE PAID ANYONE WHO CAN FURNISH EXCLUSIVE INFORMATION ON WHO SANK THE MAINE AND KILLED 258 AMERICAN SAILORS.*

* Two hundred and sixty died as a result of this explosion. After the war most of the bodies were reburied in Arlington Cemetery, the mast of the battleship being erected as a marker.

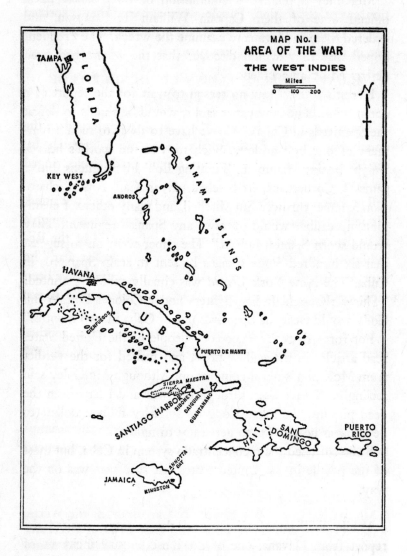

MAP No. 1
AREA OF THE WAR
THE WEST INDIES

Miles
0   100   200

McKinley appointed a commission of three senior naval officers, one of them Captain William T. Sampson, and ordered them to Havana to examine the wreck. The President hoped that they would discover that the *Maine* had been destroyed by an accident.

Hearst's *Journal* saw no reason to wait for the report of a commission. The newspaper said it would be simple to defeat the Spaniards in Cuba. "All we have to do is to send a regiment of our best athletes. Such men as the world's heavyweight boxing champion, 'Fighting Bob' Fitzsimmons, boxer James J. Corbett, expert baseball player 'Cap' Anson, champion hammer thrower Jim Mitchell, and many others of championship caliber would overawe any Spanish regiment. They would scorn Spanish bullets." The paper went on to suggest that six hundred Sioux Indians be sent to scalp Spaniards in Cuba. The New York *World* was equally rabid. It printed: "Thirty thousand Indian fighters under Colonel Buffalo Bill Cody would clear the Spaniards out of Cuba in two months."

For forty days the 73,000,000 people of the United States read articles in the yellow press, and waited for the verdict from McKinley's naval commission. Although McKinley said feelingly, "I have been through one war and I have seen the dead pile up," he asked Congress for fifty million dollars to be spent as he saw fit—to get ready to fight.

Spain softened the reconcentrado system in Cuba, but most of the people in the United States felt sure war was on the way.

While William McKinley and the country awaited the report from Havana, one of the most unusual incidents of the impending war took place. With almost every newspaper in the United States demanding a fight against Spain, the President realized that sooner or later he would probably bow to the clamor. It occurred to him that he and the War Department (today called the Department of the Army) knew precious little about the situation in Cuba. Two questions plagued him: *How much help could the Cuban rebels give, and where would be the best place for American soldiers to land?* Two U.S. Army officers had been dispatched to Cuba to gain this information and had failed.

McKinley sent for the chief of the Bureau of Intelligence, Colonel Arthur Wagner. "Wagner, I want information—up-to-date—about Cuba. I think the best way to get it is to send a man to make contact with the rebel leader, General García. He's somewhere in the jungles of Cuba, isn't he?"

"To the best of my knowledge, yes, sir."

"Where am I going to find a man, Colonel, who can carry a message to him?"

"Sir, we have in my bureau a West Point graduate named Rowan. He knows a lot about Cuba." The colonel told the President that Rowan and Professor Ramsey, of Columbia University, had written a book, *The Island of Cuba.* "I think Lieutenant Rowan is the man. I believe he can get to García and come back." *

"Is it possible to contact García by mail or telegraph?"
"No, sir."

That day Lieutenant Rowan reported to Colonel Wagner in the Washington Army and Navy Club. While they were at lunch, the colonel said, "When does the next boat leave for Jamaica?"

Rowan thought the colonel was joking, but he got up and went to the lobby desk. In a few minutes he was back. "The next boat," he said, "is the steamer *Adirondack*. It sails from New York tomorrow noon."

---

* At the time, Andrew S. Rowan had seventeen years service in the Army. Promotion in the 1890's, as described in the song "Benny Havens," was very slow.

"Can you take that ship?" The colonel leaned intently across the table.

"Why—yes."

"Then get ready to board it. Catch a train out of here tonight."

After lunch Wagner outlined Rowan's mission. "You are to go to Kingston, Jamaica, at once. Check in there with our consul. I will arrange by cable for him to help you get to Cuba. Go to General García. I don't know where he is."

Rowan's sharp nose wrinkled a bit. "Yes, sir."

The colonel told Rowan that President McKinley wanted information about the Spanish troops on the island—their number, quality, location, morale, and the character of their officers. He wanted to know how they were armed. Also, how were the rebels equipped? How long could they hold out? What kind of assistance did they need? And the President wanted to know General García's recommendation for a landing place in case the United States Army was sent to Cuba.

Lieutenant Rowan took a long breath.

"Did you ever hear of Nathan Hale?" the colonel asked.

"Yes, sir."

"Well, when the British caught Hale in 1776 they damned him as a spy and hanged him. The Spaniards catch you and you'll be lucky if they only place a noose around your neck. They're experts in torture. If they lay their hands on you you won't even have time to make a statement—like Nathan Hale."

Rowan caught a night train out of Washington, but he made sure he was on one that left a few minutes after midnight; he was superstitious about starting a journey on a Friday. The date was April 9, 1898.

In New York he boarded the ship *Adirondack*, and in three days he landed in Jamaica. The United States consul told him that he had already sent a message to García that "Rowan of Washington, a man of confidence," was on the way.

The Consul produced a guide, Gervacio Sabio, a fierce-looking Spaniard. "Sabio can get you through to García, if anyone can," he said. "He is an exiled Spaniard and he hates them. I trust him completely."

Rowan stepped into Sabio's carriage and in nine hours, using two relays of horses, the two men covered the seventy miles across Jamaica.

At dusk on the north shore, on the edge of a coconut grove at Annotto Bay, Sabio led Rowan to a fishing boat rigged with sail and manned by two members of the junta. Sabio gave the command, *"Navegue al norte noroeste hacia Ojo del Toro!"* ("Sail north-northwest for the Eye of the Bull!") It was hard for Rowan to relax in the tiny fishing boat.

At noon the next day the Sierra Maestra range in Cuba looked like a low, faint-blue fence, and two hours later it resembled a forbidden green wall. It was beautiful. Its battlements, eight thousand feet high, stretched to the east for a hundred miles. The mountain Ojo del Toro looked like a friendly beacon.

Three miles offshore, Sabio ordered the sails furled, the anchor dropped. He passed hand lines and bait to Rowan and the two members of the crew. "If we run for the shore," Sabio said, "we are lost. The patrol boats will pick us up. Now we are poor fishermen."

In an hour a patrol launch flying the yellow-and-red-striped flag of Spain chugged by, two modern machine guns mounted on the bow. "What are you catching?" the skipper of the launch shouted.

"Nothing, not even a nibble," yelled Sabio. "Amigo, the miserable fish are worse than the rebels."

The sun broiled Rowan and his friends, but Sabio made no effort to sail for the shore. "We are truly fishing for a living," he grinned.

At dark Sabio opened a locker and handed Rowan a revolver. The Spaniard equipped himself with an antique rifle. The sailboat eased for the beach. When it touched bottom Sabio and Rowan waded ashore and disappeared into the jungle. Rowan knew that his life was in the hands of Sabio, a man he had known for only a day and a half.

In the morning they walked westward through the dank forest, just out of sight of the shore. It was the hardest walking Andrew Rowan had ever done. Every type of insect attacked. The two men avoided a village, and, after thirty hard miles, the second morning found a jungle trail to the interior. At times, when they heard horses pounding along the winding path, they leaped for the jungle and lay down. There seemed to be no air. Rowan was wringing wet with perspiration, and clouds of mosquitoes and bugs, kinds he had never seen, feasted on him.

At daybreak on the eighth day of their jungle trek they heard firing. The question was: Was it friend or foe? Sabio hid the American lieutenant and walked down the trail. When he returned he had two hundred cavalrymen with him. "Friends," he said to Rowan. "They will escort us to General García. He is fighting on the Río Cauto."

At García's headquarters Sabio identified Rowan, but there was a cool note in the air. García would not see him and no one would talk to him. Sabio interceded, and in a little while he explained to Rowan, "*Señor Teniente* [Lieutenant], a mistake. From Jamaica to the general the message was, 'A *confidence man* from the United States is on the way.' I persuaded them you are a *man of confidence*."

García's appearance shocked Rowan. The big, bulky general looked as old as the hills. A white handlebar moustache and a white beard hid much of his face. In the middle of his forehead was a deep cleft. Clapped on his head was a tattered straw hat with a turned-down brim—the kind Mark Twain's king wore in *The Adventures of Huckleberry Finn*. A pistol and a cartridge belt sagged at his waist. His white uniform was soiled with dirt, and his trousers were thrust into black leather leggings that had been cut by thorns of the jungle. Rowan saluted.

In the general's tent Rowan explained his mission, and after he had asked *his* questions, García withdrew. Rowan waited for two hours, then the revolutionary general returned. With him were three rebel officers.

"Presidente McKinley asks too many questions for one man to answer," García said, "so I send him three." He placed his hand on the shoulder of one of the three staff officers. "This man is a specialist on Butcher Weyler. He even knows what the Butcher will think. This next *hombre* can answer any questions about the island and its people. This officer, Dr. Vieta, knows all that anyone knows about tropical diseases, something important to anyone who fights in our jungles."

Then General García detailed his need for arms, especially artillery that could knock down blockhouses. He said that he needed rifles of one caliber to replace the hodgepodge of weapons his soldiers were carrying. He talked of the hard problem of attacking the Spanish *trochas* and of the cruelty of the Spaniards.

"The trochas," the general explained, "are barriers that control the movement of the population. When you build a trocha you build a wide road, cut it through the jungle, one hundred and fifty to two hundred yards wide. One of them stretches out for over fifty miles. Then you border it with barbed wire fences. You build blockhouses along it and patrol it with soldiers. Sometimes we crash through. Gómez crossed a trocha last November with six hundred men. It cost him twenty-seven lives with three times that in wounded."

The general described the Spanish *fortinas*, blockhouses, death traps for assaulting infantry. He said they held about fifty soldiers. They had a cellar where men could stand and fire through loopholes at ground level. Other soldiers, standing on planks, could fire through loopholes about five feet above the ground. The walls of heavy beams were double thickness, with a crushed-stone filler.

García spoke of the beatings the Spanish administered to relatives of the rebel soldiers and how the Spaniards had raided a field hospital to murder wounded guerrillas.

When he was through talking, he treated Rowan to a supper of barbecued beef. At the end of the meal the lieutenant thanked the general and said he would give the information to the President.

After four trying days Rowan and his three companions reached a bay near Puerto Manatí, where they embarked at night in a cockleshell of a sailboat. It had sails made of a small tent and gunny sacks, and measured about 104 cubic feet in volume. After a voyage of 150 miles the four emissaries arrived at Andros Island in the Bahamas, where they caught a steamer for the Florida Keys.

The three Cubans and Rowan arrived in Washington and reported to Colonel Wagner. Thirty-five days had passed since Rowan had said good-bye to the colonel. He was tired from the strain and from the 180 miles in the Cuban jungle. Colonel Wagner hailed him. When Wagner sent word to the President that Rowan was back, McKinley welcomed the lieutenant at the White House, thanked him, and introduced him to the Cabinet. This was the greatest day in Rowan's life.

One year later the Illinois author, Elbert Hubbard, wrote an inspirational story, *A Message to García*, about Rowan's exploit. The booklet stressed Andrew Rowan's initiative and pointed out that when he was given the difficult mission he did not ask questions but left to do the job. Forty million copies of the booklet were sold. It was translated into almost every language and appeared in school readers for American children.

While Andrew Rowan was on his assignment, tension mounted in both Madrid and Washington. The Hearst press became even more fiery. Hearst invented the phrase that was placed on a million lapel buttons, "Remember the *Maine* and to hell with Spain!" Patriotic organizations held torchlight parades with bands knocking out a parody of a new tune, "There'll Be a Hot Time in Old Cuba Tonight." You could feel the breath of the coming war.

War was on the way, but the U.S. Army of 28,000 well-trained men was scattered in small detachments from Alaska to Florida. Its soldiers lived a hard, boring existence, sparked every now and then by periods of excitement. Second Lieutenant Charles Booth of Vermont, one year out of West Point, wrote his mother in 1872 about life in the foothills of the Rockies at a frontier army post in Montana territory:

Fort Burton is an old rickety tumble down affair built of adobe. The Garrison numbers 62 men, including officers. There are 30 inhabitants in the city of Burton. . . . They need a Chaplain sadly here. Church service is unknown. Sunday is a day of rest from manual labor at the Post and only there. The stores in the city are open as usual and the men drink and gamble. . . . Tell Johnny I will get the bows and arrows for him as soon as the Indians begin to come in here for the winter, but for him not to look for them before next summer when the boats begin to move on the river.

Booth survived Fort Burton and won a Silver Star Citation for bravery in Cuba.

On the frontier, the tiny American Army could function

without a General Staff to aid the Commander in Chief, the commissary department could supply food not available locally, and the quartermaster and medical departments could furnish clothing and medical care—all this with only 258 officers. However, when war broke in 1898, these vital parts of the army were inadequate. In addition, many of the army's weapons were antiques, and most of the soldiers were given black powder instead of the new smokeless powder used by the Spanish. Ahead of the United States Army, Regulars and volunteers, lay a most challenging task.

One branch of the army expanded with extraordinary care. This was the Medical Corps. It took pains to commission only competent doctors. Some contract doctors were hired. Candidates for commissions were thoroughly examined in medical science. On one of the examining boards in Washington was a talented doctor, a little known major, Walter Reed. This kind and courteous physician was already interested in tropical fever.

In the U.S. Senate, Senator Redfield Proctor, of Vermont, who had visited Cuba, rose to speak. He was effective because his speech was different. He did not yell in blood-and-thunder style, but described calmly the horrors he—and Clara Barton—had seen on the beautiful island. He told of the effect of the reconcentrado policy, of people torn from their homes, of living skeletons crawling, trying to find bits of food. He said, "Little children are still walking about with arms and chest terribly emaciated, eyes swollen, and abdomen bloated to three times the natural size. . . . Every town and village is surrounded by a trench and a barbed wire fence on the outerside. . . . Every railroad station . . . has an armed guard. Every freight train has an armored freight car, loop-holed for musketry. . . . The Spaniards have driven the people into the towns and have burned their dwellings."

But there was no sharp action in the White House. McKinley was still hoping for peace and trying, through diplomatic channels, to have Spain correct her mistakes on the island. And it was becoming obvious to Americans that Wall Street and "Mark" Hanna, McKinley's wealthy campaign manager and close advisor, wanted no war. "We are not prepared for war," McKinley repeated over and over. Excitement rose to a fever pitch. At a Gridiron Dinner given by the press in Washington, Roosevelt shook his fist and shouted, "We will have this war for the freedom of Cuba in spite of the timidity of the commercial interests!" Later the author Joseph Bishop wrote, "Teddy Roosevelt's voice stirred the country like the sound of a trumpet." In Virginia, McKinley and Hanna were burned in effigy. No one could say definitely then or later how much effect the yellow press had in promoting hysteria, but some politicians were stirred to make wild statements. Senator Henry Cabot Lodge, distinguished Senator from Massachusetts, a close friend of Roosevelt's who also wanted war, said that he had no doubt but that the *Maine* "was blown up by a government mine, fired by or with the connivance of Spanish officials." This sounded as if it came from one of Hearst's editorial rooms. People in the principal cities across the country responded to the excitement by trying to enlist in the Army, but there was no machinery to receive them.

Eight days after Proctor's potent speech the report of the naval commission arrived in Washington from Havana. It was impossible for Captain Sampson's commission, its expert divers and armor specialists, to fix the responsibility for the disaster that wrecked the *Maine* and took 260 lives. The commission reported that the battleship had been sunk by a submarine mine, but it was sure of little else. The Spanish investigated the wreck and said the disaster was an accident resulting from an explosion in the ship's forward magazine.

Whatever the truth of the matter, the American public held that the Spanish were to blame. The question of war or peace was now up to President McKinley.

Suddenly there was a tiny ray of hope. Spain not only recalled Butcher Weyler but promised reforms. The American minister in Spain cabled the President that American demands could be met.

Although he had "seen the dead pile up," President McKinley was swept along with popular sentiment in spite of the last-minute news. He failed to keep the country out of war. He was not as strong as he looked. The pressure to fight, coupled with his fear that if he did not lead toward war he would lose the leadership of his party, caved him in. He sent a message to Congress asking for authorization to use the Army and Navy in Cuba.

On April 22, 1898, Congress passed an act authorizing the enlistment of volunteer troops. The President called for 125,000 volunteers. On April 24 Spain declared war, and Congress retorted by saying a state of war had existed since April 21. At the last minute Senator Henry M. Teller, who was an expansionist, surprised everyone by introducing an amendment not in character with his previous ideas. His amendment pledged that the United States would *not* annex Cuba. In the flurry the amendment passed without even an argument. In the end this was the document that prevented the United States from annexing the troublesome isle.

Excitement in Congress was terrific. When war was declared, one Representative sang "The Battle Hymn of the Republic"; others sang "Dixie." "Fighting Joe" Wheeler, Congressman from Georgia, a former Confederate cavalry general, was wildly enthusiastic. He stood up and howled the Rebel Yell. Groups of congressmen sang, "We'll hang General Weyler to a sour apple tree as we go marching on."

War seemed like a great picnic, a modern filibuster, to

thousands of Americans. Sherwood Anderson, American literary genius from Ohio, described in his *Memoirs* how he and many other young Americans felt:

We were boys of a Middle-Western country town, farmers' sons, merchants' sons, young town roughs, gentle, quiet boys. Our hearts did not ache for the people of the island of Cuba. Our hearts ached for adventure. We wanted most of all to go to see the world, go into new strange places. . . . My heart leaped.

These boys joined an army that was not ready. However, the navy was. One reason for its readiness lay in two books on sea power by Captain Alfred T. Mahan, U.S. Navy. These books were among the most influential of the age. Mahan's theory stated it was vital for a nation to control the seas. He argued persuasively that the life of a nation at war depended upon mastery of the shipping lanes, and that for this a nation needed powerful battleships. "You can control the shipping lanes no other way," Mahan said.

His thesis had led to the construction of eight powerful battleships whose main turrets mounted guns twelve inches in diameter that could fire heavy projectiles four miles. To sink fast torpedo boats or craft that managed to get in close, the battleships had guns with bores eight inches wide and some smaller armament. So that the crews and machinery would be protected, the ships had sides of steel armor plate eighteen inches thick and deck armor of three inches.

Roosevelt, who believed implicitly in Captain Mahan, was sure that the crisis demanded that battleships and armored cruisers be assembled on the Atlantic coast. Consequently the Navy Department, back in March, 1898, ordered the battleship *Oregon* to undertake a fifteen-thousand-mile voyage from its home base in Puget Sound to the Caribbean.

When Captain Charles E. Clark of the *Oregon* received this critical order, he assembled his crew. He read the order and explained the necessity. He said the two months' voyage would surely try every man aboard. "There will be a water problem," he explained. "We can't use salt water in the boilers. Therefore, the water ration will be cut." He went on to tell the crew that the roughest seas in the world are often at the tip of South America. To be ready in case Spanish warships were encountered, the captain said that guns would be kept loaded, that gun crews would sleep close by.

"We meet the Spanish fleet and they'll whip the socks off us," he continued. "There'll be double watches." He explained to the "black gang"—stokers at the furnaces—that on this trip they would meet the challenge of their lives. The *Oregon*'s crew responded with three cheers for its captain. The battleship hoisted its anchor.

Prayers for the safety of the ship were offered in many American churches. The entire nation was interested in the cruise of the *Oregon*.

Suddenly, after war was declared, action shifted quickly halfway around the globe to Hong Kong Harbor. A United States naval squadron lay at anchor in that Chinese port, a squadron that many Americans did not even know about.

Back in February the squadron commander had been warned by cable:

DEWEY, HONGKONG, CHINA

. . . KEEP FULL OF COAL. IN THE EVENT OF WAR WITH SPAIN, YOUR DUTY WILL BE TO SEE THAT THE SPANISH SQUADRON DOES NOT LEAVE THE ASIATIC COAST. . . . AND THEN OFFENSIVE OPERATIONS IN THE PHILIPPINES. . . .

ROOSEVELT

4 DEWEY AT MANILA BAY

THE experienced officer on the bridge of the United States
cruiser *Olympia* in busy Hong Kong harbor possessed
a background equal to almost any mission that Teddy Roosevelt and the Navy Department could devise. This was George
Dewey of Vermont.

Dewey had been on his own since he was fourteen. At that
age he wanted to leave home to go to sea, but his father
persuaded him it was not a good idea, that to succeed in the
modern world he needed education. They "compromised,"
and George entered the fine military academy at Norwich.
Its Spartan life prepared him for the next hard step: the life
of a midshipman at the Naval Academy. In his *Autobiography* you can almost feel his pride about his father's words
when he told him good-bye at Annapolis. "George, you are
on your own now. I have done as much for you as I can."
These were words young Dewey liked.

George Dewey had a strong urge to be famous. He did
not have a fine physique—he was short and had a narrow

chest—but he possessed an ambition that gathered momentum. He liked adventure and to be in the center of things. Before he went to Annapolis he once attracted attention to himself by walking down the statehouse steps in Montpelier blind-folded, and on another occasion he drove his father's horse and wagon through the flooded Winooski River. He was a youngster who was willing to take risks and action for thrills and notoriety.

With Midshipman Dewey at the Naval Academy were three other unusual young men—all of whom would help change the maps of the world: Alfred Mahan, studious son of a West Point professor; Winfield Schley, a good-natured Southerner from Maryland; and modest William Sampson from Palmyra, New York.

Dewey quickly adjusted to a midshipman's life. For a boy who disliked studies, he did surprisingly well, graduating number five in a class of fifteen. When this class was sworn in as midshipmen, it had been sixty strong.

The excellent background Dewey received at Annapolis was strengthened after he graduated because he sailed the seas under stern captains who had fought in the War of 1812. He made good as an ensign. The captains liked him because he would climb aloft in a gale with the seamen to help unfurl sail. Danger seemed to attract him.

When the Civil War ripped the nation apart, Dewey was twenty-four. He was most anxious to fight, but his first as-signment on the ancient side-wheeler *Mississippi*, a ship that did its part in the blockade of the Southern states, was trying and boring. This duty made the combat he hoped for seem like a mirage. The blockade was hard, tiresome work, with long hours on watch and little sleep. When lookouts sighted Confederate blockade runners, the *Mississippi* thrashed after them in hopes of a fight, but the sleek Southern ships showed their heels and sailed out of range over the horizon.

In 1862 Lieutenant Dewey proved he was a daredevil. The old side-wheeler was caught in a bad position at Vicksburg, where Confederate shore batteries sent plunging shot ripping through the decks. Southern sharpshooters on shore picked off sailors and Marines in the rigging. The *Mississippi* was doomed. She got out of control and smashed into a mud bar, where she was an even simpler target for the Confederate gunners. The crash of the cannon balls through the ship sounded like a thunderstorm that had descended to the level of the river. Splinters showered the deck. When the captain ordered, "Abandon ship!" the crew leaped to place the wounded in small boats and to escape. Cannon balls that missed the ship sprayed the men in the boats with geysers of water.

Dewey, now a lieutenant and the ship's executive officer, was in the third lifeboat to get away, and as the little craft shot out into the river he feared he had left too soon. He shouted commands for the oarsmen to pull back to the stricken ship. When the sailors refused, he pulled two pistols from his belt and made them return. "There may still be wounded below," he shouted. "Wait!"

He scrambled up the ship's side, and in the dim light below decks he found a wounded sailor and carried him to the row-boat. Then he located a mattress, ripped it open, dashed coal oil on it from a nearby lantern, and set the mattress on fire. When the blaze started to consume the *Mississippi*, Dewey let the oarsmen pull out into midstream and to the west bank and safety. This was the man in command of the Asiatic Squadron when the *Maine* blew up.

For all his boldness and bravery, Commodore George Dewey was not popular with his contemporaries. At sixty-one his craving for fame burdened him even more than ever. His ambition was a goad. When the yellow press was yelping for war, he moaned to a friend in Montpelier, "I hate to think of getting old, of facing retirement. I dislike war, but unless there is one I shall go down as just another name in the records."

When he heard that a vacancy existed at the top of the Asiatic Squadron, he determined to get it and to let nothing stand in the way. Many naval officers would have liked to have this command far away from the control of Washington, especially when there was a strong chance that the Asiatic Squadron might see independent action. Dewey, learning that Commodore Howell, a classmate, was a leading contender for the position, hurried to see Theodore Roosevelt and asked for his help. Roosevelt was flattered, and he felt Howell was too cautious for the position.

"Do you know any senators?" Roosevelt asked.

When Dewey said he knew Senator Proctor of Vermont, Roosevelt suggested that he seek the Senator's help. Because of the influence of the Senator, and with Roosevelt working backstage, Dewey received the coveted position.

Numbers of senior naval officers were upset over the appointment, but Dewey cared little for what his contemporaries thought. On his arrival in the Far East he ran his flag up the mast of the cruiser *Olympia*. He knew he would face hard problems, so he started to work. He assembled his fleet of six warships and three supply ships and labored to improve the vessels and the crews. He made sure that extra ammunition would be shipped at once from Hawaii and the United States; he arranged to get coal from every possible source, even as far away as Cardiff, Wales; he caused the white ships to receive war paint of battleship gray; and he assembled all the reading material, charts and maps that he could on the Philippines and its waters and studied them.

It was impossible to hide all of this activity in busy Hong Kong Harbor. That Dewey was preparing for war—in the Philippines—was an open secret. In upper-class clubs in Hong

Kong, his officers were offered bets that they would be defeated by the Spanish fleet, but nothing seemed to bother Dewey. His men felt confident, even though they knew that rumors and information about the squadron would be cabled to the Philippines. The sailors believed in Dewey. They appreciated his spirit and the businesslike way he was putting the squadron in shape to fight.

When news of the sinking of the *Maine* arrived in a brief cable, Dewey and his men were so interested they chipped in money so the full story could be put in a cable for them.

Finally, on April 24, 1898, the message that Dewey had long expected arrived:

WAR HAS COMMENCED BETWEEN THE UNITED STATES AND SPAIN. PROCEED AT ONCE TO THE PHILIPPINES. CAPTURE OR DESTROY THE SPANISH FLEET.

LONG

Dewey conferred with his captains and the anchors came up. On April 27, with the band on *Olympia* playing a military march, the flagship led the fleet away from Hong Kong. Behind her in column steamed the cruisers *Baltimore*, *Raleigh* and *Concord*, with the gunboat *Petrel*. The three supply ships followed. Dewey's fleet had no big ships; the largest was under six thousand tons. Particularly important were the supply ships because, with every country in the Far East except the Philippines neutral, there was no place closer than Hawaii—seven thousand miles away—to obtain supplies. This was the start of a six-hundred-mile cruise, with disaster or fame waiting in the Philippines. With every turn of the propeller the destiny of the United States was changing.

On the third day, Dewey's lookouts sighted Cape Bolinao in western Luzon. Dewey was extremely anxious because he was not sure where the Spanish fleet was, so he sent three cruisers to investigate Subic Bay, thirty-five miles north of

Manila. The report, "No enemy in Subic Bay," relieved his nerves somewhat. He explained later that he was not anxious to rush into Manila Harbor and leave unexplored a hiding place such as Subic Bay, from which Spanish ships could charge from the rear.

The fleet approached Manila in the darkness. George Dewey now had a choice of running the gauntlet through one of the two entrances to the bay. He chose the little-used Boca Grande, the "Great Mouth." Both passages, he knew, were fortified. He did not fear submarine mines. He thought the water so deep in the Boca Grande that it would challenge the most skillful mine layers of any nation to place mines there effectively, and he guessed that, even though the Spaniards made a great to-do about requiring merchant ships to take a zigzag course through this passage, talk of large numbers of mines in the Boca Grande entrance was so much smoke. He was willing to take a chance, and in the back of his mind must have been the words of his hero, Admiral David G. Farragut, at Mobile, "Damn the torpedoes! Full speed ahead!"

What did worry Dewey were modern coast-defense guns guarding the passages. Of his cruisers only his flagship carried armor. *Olympia* was a protected cruiser; she carried light armor at vulnerable spots. The advantage of the light cruisers —more speed and a longer cruising radius—now seemed a handicap. Lack of deck armor would let plunging fire from the heights of Corregidor and from other well-placed guns tear through the decks and the bottoms.

It was ten at night when the flagship slipped into the passage. It was hot, a light rain falling. No lights were visible in the fleet except a carefully hooded light on the stern of each vessel that served as a guide for the following ship. Suddenly soot in the smokestack of the supply ship *McCulloch* caught fire. In a few minutes a signal rocket arched into the

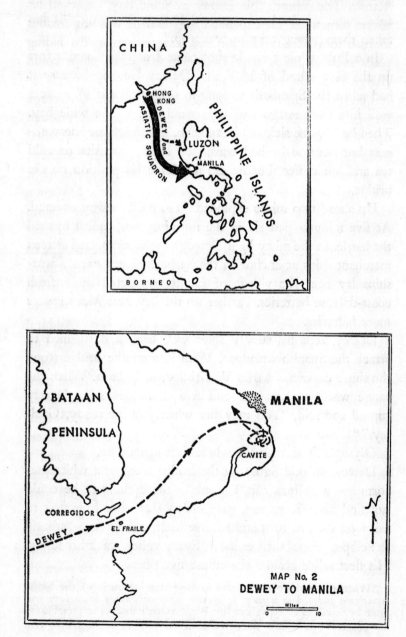

MAP No. 2
DEWEY TO MANILA

sky from Corregidor. Mr. Stickney, volunteer aide who wrote an account of the battle, quoted Dewey as saying, "It has taken them a long time to wake up."

In a little while a single shot came from the Spanish fort on the tiny island of El Fraile. Dewey laughed because it had taken the Spaniards so long to open fire. His ships were well into the passage and soon would be in the wide bay. Then he became sick at his stomach, not only from nervousness but because he had consumed large quantities of cold tea and hot coffee, but he did not leave his position on the bridge.

Up ahead two mines exploded. "Go on!" Dewey ordered. At five minutes past six in the morning the Spanish opened the battle. In the misty light Dewey's lookouts spotted sixteen merchant ships at anchor in the harbor. Eleven enemy warships lay near the village of Cavite, protected by Spanish coast-defense batteries. Farther up the bay near Manila were more batteries.

Dewey kept his supply ships well back and steamed to attack the Spanish squadron. With him on the bridge stood the ship's captain, Charles V. Gridley, of Indiana. When the range was between four and five thousand yards, Dewey turned and said, "You may fire when you are ready, Gridley." *

Olympia fired, then the whole fleet opened up.

Dewey, an odd figure on the bridge wearing a white uniform and a golfer's cap, because in the excitement he could not find his officer's cap, gave orders that caused his fleet to sail west then to turn and reverse itself, sailing east—"around the ellipse," naval men called it. Every volley was a broadside. His fleet sailed around the ellipse five times.

---

* When this order was reported in newspaper accounts of the battle, Americans adopted it eagerly. It became a famous saying, used over and again by people in every walk of life. For instance, a baseball umpire, instead of saying, "Play ball!" would repeat Dewey's remark.

The Americans were outnumbered in ships, but they were superior in weight of metal that could be fired at any instant. The Spanish ships were smaller.

Spanish shells shrieked over the American ships. Although he was maneuvering smartly, Dewey felt bad because his war vessels were not firing accurately. Gunners on the *Olympia* sent him a message asking him to sail closer to the enemy. When he reduced the distance to two thousand yards his shells raked the modern Spanish cruiser *Reina Cristina*. Smoke filled the bay. It was hard for range finders and gunners to see. Suddenly out of the smoke darted a torpedo boat straight for the *Olympia*. Mr. Stickney warned the commodore, and Dewey answered sharply, "Well, you look out for her! Don't bother me with torpedo boats! Tell me when you've sunk her."

Quick-firing guns sent the torpedo boat to the bottom.

Even though the *Reina Cristina* (displacement 3,520 tons) was smaller than the *Olympia* (5,870 tons), the Spanish ship sailed bravely to challenge the American flagship, but had to turn back because of the pounding. On the bridge of the Spanish warship stood Admiral Montojo and his two sons, who were his aides. With the guns of the shore batteries firing hard, though at long range, to protect her, the Spanish ship became a chief target. A shell pierced her, exploded the magazine, and wrecked the ship. Seventy-five percent of the ship's complement died, a loss of 130 people. The Spanish admiral transferred his flag to a smaller warship and continued to fight.

After three hours of battle, Dewey received a report that ammunition was running short. He ordered a withdrawal to the middle of the bay "for breakfast." Mr. Stickney reported the intense feeling of the gunners on the *Olympia*: "Don't take us out of action now! To hell with breakfast!" Dewey's real reason for withdrawing was to order a precise count of ammunition. This was an anxious moment. If ammunition was short the mission could not be fulfilled.

There was enough ammunition, and after breakfast Commodore Dewey brought his warships back and pounded the enemy for two more hours. The Spaniards fought until they could fight no longer. Their ships were down or in flames. Not only was the Spanish fleet outclassed in armament, but it was outgunned by American sailors and was put completely out of action. From one of the forts, at 12:30 P.M., international code signal flags were hauled up a flag pole. They read, "*We Surrender.*" Cheers went up from Dewey's sailors.

The battle brought death to 167 Spaniards and wounded about 250. Dewey was delighted to find that his loss was only seven slightly wounded.

The commodore did not trust his enemy. To make sure that no Spanish ship hidden in the backwaters near Manila escaped, he ordered the tiny gunboat *Petrel* to demolish torpedo boats near the city. When the *Petrel* returned with six captured boats in tow, the Americans cheered.

The next day the rest of the forts surrendered, and Dewey was master of Manila Bay. He sent men ashore to the forts to place bands of gun cotton around the coast defense guns to blow them up. His task now was to inform the Navy Department of his victory, but the Spanish Governor in Manila would not let him use the cable to Hong Kong, so Dewey had a ship drag its anchor over the cable and cut it. To send his message, he dispatched the *McCulloch* all the way to Hong Kong.

When Dewey's report reached the Navy Department, Theodore Roosevelt read it and instead of telling his chief, John D. Long, first, he informed the newspapermen. There was wild excitement. Some Americans had not even a hazy idea where the Philippines were. President McKinley himself was checking Far Eastern strategy on a map cut out of a schoolbook. People were surprised. Dewey's venture had been announced only a few days before he sailed for the Philippines. A popular remark after the fight was, "The United States aimed at Cuba and hit the Philippines."

Humorist Finley Peter Dunne, writing for the Chicago *Evening Post*, had his Irish-American characters sum up the situation. Mr. Dooley remarked, "They are eight thousan' uv thim islands, with a population uv wan hundherd millyon naked savages."

"If I was Mack," said Mr. Hennessy, "I'd hist a flag over th' Ph'lippeens, an' I'd take th' whole lot iv thim."

"An' yet," said Mr. Dooley, "tis not more thin two months since ye larned they were islands or canned goods. If yer son Packy was to ask ye where th' Ph'lippeens is, cud ye give him anny good idea whether they was in Rooshia or just west iv th' thracks?"

Americans were delighted over the victory and at having a toehold on a colony. Dewey buttons appeared. Parades were formed, with brass bands up in front of the Colors. There was widespread rejoicing. Students lit bonfires on campuses and politicians made rabid speeches.

The President cabled Dewey expressing his own appreciation and the thanks of the American people. Secretary Long and many organizations sent similar messages. Then Long dispatched a cable saying that Congress sent its thanks to Dewey and the fleet, and that the President had recommended Dewey to the Senate for promotion.

Shortly George Dewey had the pleasure of hauling the two-star flag of a rear admiral up the mast of the *Olympia*. In a most unusual exchange of letters with Admiral Montojo, Dewey responded to the admiral's fear of execution by Spain (because he had lost his fleet) by sending Montojo a letter of recommendation, saying that his defense of Cavite had been "gallant in the extreme."

Admiral Dewey had served the interests of the United States, but he was now in a peculiar position. In the distance glowed the lights of Manila. He was blockading its harbor but lacked Marines and soldiers to conduct a land campaign against the Spaniards. The situation was a three-cornered puzzle. One of the sharpest elements in it was a young Filipino, Emilio Aguinaldo. This fighter against Spanish tyranny loved freedom and craved power and adventure. Because the Spaniards had been unable to defeat him, they had given him money so he would go into exile in China.

Now Aguinaldo was back and anxious to act in the cause of Philippine independence. He seemed to regard himself as a king. His initial orders to the Filipinos bore the words, "I decree that . . ."

Dewey himself misjudged matters. He did not think the Philippine rebels would fight, and he wrote this to Mr. Long. The situation was becoming so involved that President Mc-Kinley wished that Dewey had sailed from Manila bay as soon as the enemy fleet was destroyed.

A military expedition prepared to sail from San Francisco for the conquest of the Philippines. Serious trouble awaited the soldiers.

5   TURMOIL ON LAND

I**N THE** meantime there was almost as much excitement in the United States as when word arrived that Dewey said, "You may fire when you are ready, Gridley."

A million men volunteered. Veterans of the Civil War, in the South as well as the North, pleaded for a chance to serve the flag, but most of them were too old. The agitation and bustle made the war seem like a national rodeo.

Eben J. Swift wrote from Camp Alger, Virginia,

> I was appointed major with the 7th Illinois Infantry, otherwise known as "The Hibernian Riflers," an Irish regiment from the stockyards of Chicago. . . . Nearly all Irish except the band. The band is German. It can play only two tunes, "Listen to the Mocking Bird," and "The Wearing of the Green.". . . . There are no bathing facilities and the principal diet is hard tack and sow belly with the buttons on. There are box cars on the siding with food and clothing, but the outsides are unlabeled, and an officer looking for beans might find patent leather shoes. Sometimes soldiers are seen on the streets of Washington, about thirty miles away, begging for food while it lies in the cars rotting. . . . When the 2nd Tennessee Regiment arrived there was not a uniform in the regiment. . . .

Out of the storm of emotion, distressing facts were borne home to the public. The United States Army, scattered in tiny posts over wide distances, would have to leave men behind to keep peace in Indian Territory. The Army had no units larger than regiments of twelve hundred, and few officers had ever seen as many as two regiments together.

The enemy? Word from many sources placed the number of Spanish soldiers in Cuba at 160,000. They had an advantage: They knew the ground over which the war would be fought.

The National Guard's value to the United States was dubious because it varied from state to state. Although it numbered a hundred thousand men, most of its soldiers knew little of field maneuvers. They had specialized in complicated close-order drills, guard mount, and parade. In one regiment the soldiers were hardly familiar with their rifles. They were going to war and had fired less than seven rounds per man. In many units of the National Guard discipline, so essential in battle, was nonexistent. Guard officers were usually elected. There were as many different "armies" in the National Guard as there were states. One of the big problems was: Could the National Guard serve outside the country? No one knew, because the Guard was controlled by the governors of the states rather than by the United States.

There was a strong feeling in the National Guard against West Point graduates because many of them had reputations for being martinets. Walter Millis, American journalist, wrote in his historical study on the war, "The Martial Spirit," ". . . West Point martinets were scarce [but] they were later to prove valuable."

Congress did not want a large Regular Army, so it merely doubled its size.

To overcome the need for more soldiers Congress passed a bill that let National Guard units serve as volunteer units as long as state governors approved. The number of volunteers was raised from 125,000 to 267,000. This alone multiplied the problems because the War Department was swamped with details as to how to form an army, equip and train it. Sanitary conditions in the hastily-put-together camps in the South, where the Army was assembling, were typified by those at Camp Alger.

This camp was named for the head of the War Department, Russell Alexander Alger, wealthy lumberman who once was a popular Governor of Michigan. He was blamed for the Army's state of unreadiness, especially as the war proceeded.

Alger had had an unusual military background. When the bullets began to crack and the cannons started to fire in the Civil War, Alger sought danger. He had enlisted as a private, and had been oustanding in the lower ranks. On the way to the rank of major general he had proved his bravery numerous times. When General Philip H. Sheridan and his Michigan and Iowa cavalry were hard pressed at Booneville, Mississippi, in 1862, Captain Alger with ninety picked horsemen galloped around to the Confederates' rear and recklessly charged three thousand men to help win the battle. He was wounded, taken prisoner, and escaped, all in the same day.

Alger was wounded four times. But after the silver eagles of a colonel were pinned to his collar, a different kind of trouble began. At the start, Alger had commanded his regiment efficiently, and he led it under Sheridan in the Shenandoah Valley. Suddenly court-martial charges were preferred against him for being absent without leave. The charges were signed by General Custer and endorsed by three other senior officers. Alger countered by saying he had been sick in Maryland at the time, and that he was also on duty in Washington. A fog drifted over the affair and Alger escaped trial.

As Secretary of War thirty-two years later, Mr. Alger was far from the star he had been on the battlefields. He was neither forceful nor direct; he enjoyed intrigue, failed to cut red tape, and did not back his commanding general. Alger wasted time by making himself available to hundreds of applicants for officers' commissions from every state in the Union. But he did have a sense of humor. In his story of the war he described a card which one applicant for office presented:

> *Sec. of War, please see Major ... of the 6th Md. Regt., and give him good arms if possible.*
>
> A. Lincoln
>
> *Oct., 7, 1862*

As the war went on, President McKinley tired of Mr. Alexander Alger. Once, in his mild way, the President complained to Alger that his effort was inconsistent. Some of his trouble arose because he was unable to visualize the tremendous difficulties the army faced in expansion, in assembling, in being equipped, and in training. When the President asked him, "How soon can you put an army in Cuba?" Alger replied glibly, "We can put forty thousand men there in ten days."

Yet not all the confusion and lack of supply can be charged against Mr. Alger, who was appointed Secretary only a year before the war. Deep jealousies existed between senior officers in the Army, as they did in the Navy. Stocks of supplies such as tentage were worthless. The American people were to blame for much of the turmoil and lack of preparedness: They had given little thought or funds to the War Department or to the Army since the War Between the States. The country had been contented with the Army's role in the West, because the Army was overcoming the Indians and because the fights were miles away from population centers. Suddenly in 1898 the Army was important.

The senior general, Nelson A. Miles, had a war record

few Americans have equaled. When he was seventeen he decided to be a soldier, studying the fundamentals of a military education under a former French Army officer. At the start of the Civil War young Miles was a captain, but when he was about to lead his company into battle for the first time, he was benched because he was "too young." When he did get a chance at Fair Oaks in 1862, he was wounded and cited for bravery. He received promotion after promotion. As a colonel at Fredericksburg he almost died when he was shot through the throat. At Chancellorsville the following year, out in front of his corps helping to hold a line of obstacles against the Confederates, he was shot from his horse. This bravery beyond the call of duty won him the Medal of Honor. He received the thanks of Congress, and when his fearlessness led to his fourth wound at Petersburg, he was promoted to brigadier general. At the age of twenty-six, Miles commanded twenty-six thousand men.

After the Civil War Nelson Miles fought Indians for fifteen years, defeating the Cheyennes, Kiowas, Comanches, and Sioux, establishing himself as one of the foremost Indian fighters. He was imaginative, and he did not always "fight by the book." Once, against the Cheyennes on the Yellowstone River, he tricked the Indians into thinking that two field pieces, disguised under canvas, were parts of a wagon train. At the proper moment the canvas was thrown aside and the two cannons went into action.

Now, as commanding general of the Army in his office in the War Department with a war under way, Miles discovered that the difficulties he faced were far harder to solve than hectic action on a battlefield. His prime trouble came with his immediate superior, Secretary of War Alger. They hardly spoke because their ideas differed. Each mistrusted and disliked the other. Alger thought he needed no advice on how to run the army, since he had been a general in the Civil War.

Alger was charming, smooth and evasive. Miles was hard to get along with, vain, and at times overbearing. There was a feeling in Washington that Miles had his cap set for the Presidency.

Both men were extraordinarily handsome. General Miles, who had a love for show, liked to don his full dress uniform on important occasions and appear with his chest covered with medals. This led Roosevelt to characterize him as "merely a brave peacock."

There was nothing wrong with Miles's thinking. He wanted the Regular Army to assemble at Chickamauga Park, Georgia, where it could train as a unit. Mr. Alger disapproved. He ordered the infantry to New Orleans, Tampa, and Mobile, the cavalry and artillery to Chickamauga, and established another camp at Falls Church, Virginia.

When General Miles wrote Mr. Alger advising him that the rainy season was soon due in Cuba, that it was a "sickly season" because of deadly disease and yellow fever, and that it would be far better "to devote the summer to organizing, equipping, and drilling the volunteers [in the United States]," Alger quickly torpedoed this advice. And to make sure that the man he disliked did not gain more glory, he selected General William R. Shafter to command the forces that would land in Cuba.

The Secretary of War believed that if the Stars and Stripes were carried to the island with a show of force, Spain would withdraw without a fight. There were others who also held to his idea. Consequently, General Shafter was ordered to take five thousand Regulars, make a reconnaissance in force to Cuba, and to give all possible aid to the Rebels. He was to learn all he could about the situation on the island and to come back in a few days with an idea as to where more United States soldiers could land.

Part of the plan called for reaching the rebel General

Gómez and giving him arms and ammunition. It was thought this magnificent gesture would put new spirit into Gómez' men and would let them know that the United States was actively behind them. How large Gómez' army was no one knew.

The entire scheme appeared in the newspapers.

Hardly had General Shafter arrived in Tampa on April 29 to carry out his orders when he received a telegram from the War Department calling off the mission because the Navy Department said it could not spare the ships. The first objective would have to be the destruction of the Spanish fleet.

The day before, exciting news had flashed over the cable from American newspapermen in Spain: The Spanish fleet had disappeared from the Cape Verde Islands off the African coast. The newsmen said its course was west, but where the warships were headed no American knew.

While the Navy Department and citizens in East Coast cities from Savannah to Portland, Maine, worried about the destination of the Spanish fleet, the War Department erupted in a rush of orders. It believed enough ships were now available to land General Shafter and troops on Cuba. Consequently he was ordered to land west of Havana and to surround Havana. "When this has been accomplished," the order said, "the force can be rapidly increased and Havana deliberately approached."

The next day this order was also canceled. It was fortunate that General Shafter was of placid disposition. He took confusion in stride.

A few days later the War Department ordered twelve thousand infantrymen to proceed at once to Key West, Florida, so they could be ready to go to Cuba as soon as ships were available, but this order was voided before it could be obeyed when it was learned that there was not enough drinking water at Key West for twelve thousand men.

While the keys to the attack on Cuba were the American and Spanish fleets, the United States Army decided to conduct a search of its own for landing places along the shores in the western half of the island. A call went out for volunteers —for officers or soldiers who could sail a boat. Shortly the crews of "about fifteen or sixteen" small sailboats hoisted canvas and departed from Key West on this dangerous mission. The heaviest armaments aboard these sailboats were Springfield rifles.

Captain Russell P. Reeder, a volunteer from Cincinnati in the First Ohio Infantry and a member of the crew on one of the little sloops, said, "If the Spanish fleet had seen us we would have been gobbled up. But we sailed, and in eight days to two weeks we were all back with ideas about landing places."

The next plan in the War Department was a scheme to run arms, ammunition, and supplies ashore for the Cuban Rebels. The man selected to lead this expedition was a cavalry officer, Captain Joseph Dorst of Indiana. He was given two companies of the First Infantry Regiment and an old side-wheeler, the *Gussie*, a steamboat of Civil War vintage. Arms and ammunition were placed on board. Newspapermen applied for passage, and after they were accepted they said they did not like the name of the ship. "People will laugh about 'The *Gussie* Expedition,'" they said. Although the newspapermen complained that the name of the ship was not dramatic enough, the steamboat captain refused to change the *Gussie*'s name. "It would be bad luck," he explained.

The *Gussie* Expedition was given wide publicity in the papers, and when it arrived off the Cuban coast, hordes of people came to the water's edge to see the *americanos*. Captain Dorst asked the captain to try for a more secluded place, but the ship found itself under surveillance by a troop of Spanish cavalry. The *Gussie* put about, and at night off

Cabañas, thirty-five miles west of Havana, forty American infantrymen rowed ashore in small boats. Two tugboats carrying American newsmen steamed along to record vital events.

Captain Dorst was in the front rank. Rifle fire from the jungle greeted his party, and a newswriter from the San Francisco *Post* received a bullet in the arm. The soldiers pulled back to the steamboat, and after two more days of trying without success to find a place where they could put their arms and ammunition ashore, the *Gussie* sailed back to Tampa. Joseph Dorst laid the failure of the expedition to the publicity in the newspapers. He was probably correct.

The whereabouts and the destination of the Spanish fleet were in everyone's mind. There were almost as many rumors around as there were in Mark Twain's "The Stolen White Elephant." The Spanish warships were reported off Newfoundland, off New England, back in Cádiz, Spain, and lying in wait near the South American coast to sink the *Oregon*.

All future action depended upon the United States Navy. It was far better equipped and readier for action than the army, but the navy was having its troubles, too.

6   CONFUSION AT SEA

THE coming naval war in the Caribbean hinged on the characteristics of three men—two Americans and a Spaniard. Orders from home governments, of course, also influenced the action.

At Key West, Captain William T. Sampson, U.S.N., had "one of the most powerful fleets that ever floated in American waters" awaiting the declaration of war. He was a hard man to know, this William Sampson, but after you penetrated his reserve you liked him. He was a serious-looking, modest officer, with a nose like a ski slide. He made a habit of hard work, a habit that had started in his boyhood at Palmyra, New York, when he earned money as a laborer. In high school he was so earnest about his studies that his teachers backed him in his effort to go to the Naval Academy.

When he reported at the Academy to start his naval career, he looked like an ungainly country boy. To begin with, he did not stand out in comparison with the other midshipmen, but by graduation time Sampson ranked at the top of his class and commanded the midshipman battalion.

He liked science: physics, chemistry, metallurgy and astronomy, and when he graduated, even though the Civil War was raging, the Navy used him as a teacher at Newport, Rhode Island. In the war he did not become a hero like George Dewey, but in 1865 in Charleston Harbor he had a horrible experience.

Two years before that time, young Sampson had ridden the Union monitor *Patapsco* into Charleston harbor. The Union fleet was cautious because it knew that the Confederates had planted a network of "torpedoes"—mines—beneath the water. Four monitors, each a "cheesebox on a raft" similar to John Ericsson's *Monitor*, inched ahead of the larger warships. When the fleet was in range it fired at the Confederate forts and the city. The attack was a disappointment to the Union because only one fort was taken, another demolished, and the city remained uncaptured.

The Navy did not quit. In early 1865 the *Patapsco* had the job of trying to remove the mines in the harbor. This was dangerous because the metal globes filled with explosives were at varying depths and were connected by ropes. If a propeller fouled a hawser, a chain of mines might explode. Lieutenant Sampson was standing on the turret of the monitor where he could direct the work. Suddenly a mine blew up. The monitor plunged to the bottom like a stone, carrying sixty men with her. Fortunately, William Sampson escaped.

Thirty-three years later, after a career that had placed him as Superintendent at Annapolis and as chief of ordnance for the Navy, Captain Sampson headed the inquiry into the sinking of the *Maine*. Now aboard the armored cruiser *New York* at Key West, he commanded an imposing-looking but nondescript fleet.

Close by in the light-green water, outside of the reef, lay

the battleships *Iowa* and *Indiana*. A little farther away at anchor were ships of various types, including about forty little vessels chartered by newspapermen.

Key West was a splendid base for William Sampson's ships because from there they could steam readily for Cuba, one hundred miles away, or storm north if Spanish warships attacked an Atlantic seaboard city.

A United States fleet at Hampton Roads, Virginia, across the water from Norfolk, was also ready to sail on one hour's notice. It was called the "Flying Squadron." Even more famous than William Sampson was its commander, Winfield Scott Schley, a jaunty seadog who sported a well-kept moustache and a close-clipped Vandyke beard. Schley's eyes twinkled, and he was alert-looking. People liked him.

He had proved his bravery as a young officer in the Civil War, and twenty years afterward almost every American knew about him because he had been selected to lead a relief expedition to the Arctic to search for an army officer-explorer, Lieutenant Adolphus W. Greely. Greely had been lost in the frozen seas for almost two years. Two relief excursions had already failed. Schley took plenty of time and made double-sure that he had enough supplies before he departed to try to rescue Greely's meteorological party.

No one knew that Greely's ship had been crushed by polar ice and sunk, that sixteen of his men had died of starvation, that one had drowned, that another had been shot for stealing food, and that one or two had descended to cannibalism.

Schley traveled thirteen hundred miles into the Arctic and found Greely, arriving just in time to save the Army scientist and six men from death. When Schley brought them out, he, along with Greely, was acclaimed a hero.

The people along the Atlantic coast were delighted when Commodore Schley was chosen as the leader of the Flying

Squadron at Hampton Roads. The public had confidence that he could sail to the attack and sink any Spanish squadron. However, at fifty-nine the commodore was no longer the carefree, slashing hero that he had been in the Civil War or when he had braved the Arctic. Responsibility and age had changed him. In 1898 he was still a worthy officer who could inspire men, a hail fellow well met, but he had become a deep worrier. He was now a man who could not ride over obstacles.

The first thing that bothered him was the order from the Navy Department that his squadron must be ready to sail at an hour's notice. This meant daily coaling of his warships. Coaling ship and continual swabbing of the decks was backbreaking labor for his sailors. False alarms added to the pressure. For thirty-seven days the crews of Schley's two battleships, one armored cruiser, one protected cruiser, and one collier—*Merrimac*—were kept on a Class-A alert.

The Spanish admiral who found himself on the spot was Pascual Cervera y Topete. This man had long been groomed for a naval career, but the web of events in 1898 and his reaction to them bound him as if he were a prisoner.

When Cervera was nine, his parents decided that he should have a naval career. Consequently he was sent from his wealthy home near the southern tip of Spain to a naval school, where he stayed until he was twelve. At the age of fourteen he was given a chance in revolutionary struggles off the coast of Morocco. He fought so fearlessly that he was decorated and promoted.

At the age of twenty-three Lieutenant Cervera sailed around the Horn to fight off the coast of Peru, then served for a while as an attaché in the Spanish embassy in Washington. Four years later he saw action again in naval fights near the Peruvian coast, this time in command of a ship. His characteristics were well known—he was courteous and brave. As an admiral, Cervera looked more like a well-established banker or clergyman, with a high forehead crowned with white hair, a close-cropped white beard, and neat moustache. The main feature of his quizzical look was his kindly eyes. He was the same age as Schley.

The Spaniard took a dim view of the coming conflict with the United States. He knew that disaster was at hand and predicted it in a private letter to a cousin. During his stay in Washington as an attaché he had seen the almost unlimited power of the United States. Now the fleet was his to fight against enemies of Spain.

The admiral tried to warn the Spanish naval minister in a series of almost pathetic letters that his fleet was in disrepair. Cervera said the guns of his best cruiser were "practically useless," that coal and supplies of all kinds were low, that he had no charts of American waters, and that the machinery of some of his ships was so old that they were museum pieces. He pointed out that the artillery power of the United States Navy was greater than that of his navy by a ratio of over 2.6 to 1. Then he asked the minister what the plans were for the coming war.

In a letter beginning "My Dear Admiral and Friend," the minister revealed that he lived in a dreamworld. "Our flag is flying in Cuba," he said, "and to support it there are fourteen Spanish warships in Havana harbor. All of these are yours. . . . We shall conquer. First, because of the discipline of our crews. Next, because as soon as the action begins the nondescript American crews will desert."

Cervera countered by saying that the fourteen warships of various types in Havana Harbor were so old they were worthless.

Spanish honor seemed to be involved, and Cervera's objections were brushed aside. A council of eighteen admirals sustained the Spanish minister, and Cervera was ordered to sail for Cuba. The minister advised that the fleet of four armored cruisers and six torpedo boats could blockade the American coast in the Gulf of Mexico and stop the American fleet in the straits between Florida and Cuba. He made it look simple.

Cervera shook his head. It was almost a suicide mission. He was defeated mentally before he sailed, therefore he was a poor choice to command the fleet. He did not see a single chance of winning.

After a hard voyage west, during which there were machinery breakdowns and an exceedingly slow pace because the smallest ships had to be towed, Cervera steamed into Santiago harbor on May 19. He had not seen a single American warship.

In the meantime, American leaders agreed that before the U.S. Army could land in Cuba the Spanish fleet had to be located and sunk. Spain had fine naval bases at Havana and San Juan, Puerto Rico.

Captain Sampson had an aggressive plan to shell the forts guarding the sea entrance to Havana, then threaten the city with bombardment. "It will probably surrender," he said, "then we can attack San Juan."

Before he sailed, Sampson, a mild-spoken man, sent Secretary Long a telegram requesting that no "press associations be with the squadron." Sampson understood the value of the press to Americans, but he believed publishing orders and plans in the newspapers helped the enemy. "The *Gussie* expedition is a good example," he said.

The press boats chugged through Key West waters like ferry boats. One writer wrote that the fleet *couldn't* sail because news dispatch boats were tied to the anchor chains, rudders, and propellers. But Secretary Long could not resist the power of the press and refused to support Captain Sampson's request.

On April 21, 1898, Sampson received a telegram from the Navy Department: SPANISH FLEET HAS LEFT AFRICAN COAST, CAPE VERDES, DESTINATION UNKNOWN.

The order went on to direct Sampson to blockade 130 miles of Cuba's 2,000-mile-long northern coast near Havana. The bombardment of the city was canceled. At eight in the evening, on the heels of the order, came another telegram promoting William Sampson to rear admiral.

He ordered his fleet to assemble outside Key West at 4:30 A.M. the next morning, and at eight he hauled the two-star blue flag of a rear admiral to the top of the mast of his flagship *New York*. Every warship fired a gun in salute. Then the fleet of two battleships, six cruisers, six gunboats, six torpedo boats, one converted yacht, a collier, some tugs, and the newspapermen's boats steamed into the Straits of Florida.

Almost immediately the torpedo boats (improved monitors) ran into trouble. The rough water banged them about, and they had to be towed by the bigger ships because they could not carry enough coal for the voyage. This slowed the fleet. Life was hell on the small boats as waves washed over their decks. Towlines parted and boilers leaked. When the tug *Tecumseh* reported herself as sinking, a young graduate of the Naval Academy, Richmond Pearson Hobson, volunteered to board the tug and go below to superintend repairs. Hobson, an assistant naval constructor, sought danger.

Now Admiral Sampson received a message that war was declared. His fleet, although it was experiencing difficulty in the rough water, was in position to stop the Spanish fleet— if it came—from entering the capital city of Cuba. It was the Civil War all over again: blockade duty with long hours and hard, dull work.

There was no radio. To receive or send messages, Sampson

sent fast boats to Key West or to islands in the Caribbean
that had cable stations.

It now appeared from reports that if Admiral Sampson
sailed to Puerto Rico he could meet the Spanish warships.
(*See* Map No. 1, page 17.) So he daringly divided his fleet
and sailed for what he hoped was an attack. On the trip
heavy swells kept the sailors on the monitors miserable.
Towlines parted again and a few ships seemed in danger of
foundering.

When Admiral Sampson arrived off San Juan he was ahead
of time by four days, but of course he did not know it. All
he knew was that there were no Spanish ships in the vicinity.
He bombarded briefly the forts of the city and its naval base.
The Spaniards reported that some of the shells banged into
the town, killing women and children. After a few hours the
admiral hoisted signals and his fleet followed him back to
Havana to strengthen the blockade.

Two days later Sampson received a message that Admiral
Cervera and his ships were headed for the island of Curaçao,
just north of Venezuela. To help Admiral Sampson, the Navy
Department released the Flying Squadron. Schley and his men
were delighted to be ordered away from Hampton Roads
and the perpetual job of coaling ship. There was great excitement among the sailors, who knew that they would soon meet
the enemy.

Shortly after Commodore Schley and his squadron arrived
at Key West, Admiral Sampson steamed in on the *New York.*
One of his first jobs was to read a letter from Miss Clara
Barton of the American Red Cross. She said she had permission from the Spanish government at Madrid to take food to
the starving people of Cuba. She intimated that she trusted
the Spanish Army in Cuba and asked the admiral for permission to land under a flag of truce so she could distribute food
to the famished population.

Sampson replied, politely but firmly, that he was sure the food would never reach the needy Cubans, but would be distributed to the Spanish Army. He concluded that he could not give Clara Barton permission to break the blockade.

In a conference with Commodore Schley, William Sampson told him that Havana was blockaded and that he thought Schley's best chance to catch the enemy fleet was at Cienfuegos. (*See* Map No. 1, page 17.) "I wish you would establish the blockade there," Admiral Sampson concluded.

When Schley got his ships under way next morning, Admiral Sampson handed a slip of paper to the signal officer on the *New York*, and in a moment a signal boy wigwagged a message to Schley and his men: "*You are bound for Cienfuegos, Cuba, to bag the Dons, and may good luck go with you.*" Chaplain Harry Jones, on Schley's flagship, the armored cruiser *Brooklyn*, wrote later in his book, *A Chaplain's Experiences Ashore and Afloat*, "Our men were delighted. They chased one another around the decks, jumping highbacks." After they quieted down, many of the sailors bet one another as to which gun would fire the first shot.

Now trouble hit. Worry acted as a brake on Commodore Schley. His jovial nature was under test. As sometimes happens, a man who is a hero in one war may not be as dashing under pressure years later. Few seadogs could better Schley's record for bravery in the Civil War. His expedition into the Arctic to rescue Greely proved Schley had grit to spare. But now, thirteen years after his navigation in the Arctic ice floes, Schley worried over details. Important details, but they diverted him from driving for the mission.

The coal supply was a constant harassment. It seemed to Schley that he might run out of fuel. In the rough water of the Florida Straits, bucking the Gulf Stream, his warships were devouring coal. When he had a message wigwagged to his ships asking how much coal each had, he noted it, but to obtain the amount on hand he subtracted the amount of coal needed to steam back to Key West. He was becoming less offensive-minded with each ton of coal consumed.

Off Cienfuegos he became confused by signal lights flashed at night by the rebels. A United States naval officer on a scout ship knew of these signals but neglected to tell Schley what they were. The commodore, although he could not see into the harbor because of its narrow, winding entrance and the high hills shielding it, assumed he had Cervera blockaded. He had no thought at this time of sending a patrol ashore at night to check. If the idea occurred to him, he discarded it.

When the British ship *Adula* steamed up and asked for permission to go through the blockade, Schley gave approval for the ship to enter provided it told him the next day, when it was scheduled to come out, if Cervera's fleet was inside the harbor.

Twenty-four hours slipped by, and when the *Adula* did not return from Cienfuegos Harbor Schley *knew* he had the Dons bottled up. He tried to coal ship by having a collier pull alongside his war vessels, but the rough water made coaling almost impossible and extremely dangerous to both ships and men.

Finally, after three days of blockading the port, Commodore Schley sent Commander McCalla ashore as a scout. The commander landed thirteen miles from the harbor's entrance, and from rebels he learned that the Flying Squadron had been watching an empty nest. Cervera's fleet was not in Cienfuegos.

The commodore ordered "up anchors" and steamed at a leisurely pace for Santiago. On the afternoon of May 26 his squadron arrived there after a four-day trip. The distance was only 310 miles. While his fleet was en route, the fast converted liner *Harvard*, now a scout cruiser, steamed up with a message from Washington:

COMMODORE W. S. SCHLEY
COMMANDING THE FLYING SQUADRON
    INFORMATION INDICATES SPANISH FLEET STILL AT SANTIAGO.
    ... ASCERTAIN FACTS. DO NOT LEAVE WITHOUT DECISIVE ACTION. ...

Another message arrived for Schley by a speedy yacht:

CONFIDENTIAL REPORTS SAY SPANISH SQUADRON IS IN SANTIAGO
HARBOR. ... BLOCKADE THAT PORT.

W. T. SAMPSON
REAR ADMIRAL, U.S. NAVY

Off Santiago Harbor, Schley talked to three small American ships that were scouting for Cervera. None of them knew anything about the Spanish fleet. Through a glass the flag of Spain could be seen flying from forts guarding the entrance. Unfortunately for Schley it was like the harbor at Cienfuegos: no one could see into it from the ocean.

Lieutenant Beal, on the *Harvard*, asked his captain for permission to go ashore to make certain whether the harbor was empty or not, but either his captain or Schley disapproved the request of this brave volunteer.

Schley now sent the *Harvard* to the cable station at Kingston, Jamaica, with a message for Washington saying that his ships were low on coal and that he was sailing back to Key West. The commodore signaled his fleet and began the long journey, slightly over one thousand miles, away from the Spanish warships.

Actually he had traveled only fifty miles when the sea abated and he was able to coal ship. Then he steamed back to blockade Santiago.

Two days later, near the harbor entrance, Schley and his lookouts saw the masts of two ships. From reference books he was able to identify these as belonging to the Spanish men-of-war the *Colon* and the *María Teresa*. He also saw two Spanish torpedo-boat destroyers. To spread the news, he promptly sent a boat to cable Washington, and to celebrate he bombarded the harbor forts.

Commanding the battleship *Iowa* was one of the great leaders of the Navy, "Fighting Bob" Evans. He fumed because his ship and the rest of Schley's fleet were too far out. Captain Evans ordered that one of the *Iowa*'s guns be elevated to its highest angle, but after it had been fired the gun was put out of action temporarily. Firing from two and one-half miles out was not Fighting Bob's idea of combat.

While Schley was blockading Santiago, Admiral Sampson was back at Key West, not with his fleet but with a section of it, to receive coal and any communications from Washington. Suddenly there was excitement. The battleship *Oregon* pulled into Key West after a sixty-eight-days' voyage from San Francisco. In that day this was a remarkable speed for a trip around the Horn. Her captain, Charles Clark, boarded the *New York* and was welcomed by Sampson. He told the admiral that the battleship was in amazingly good condition and described the *Oregon*'s trial by tempest as it navigated the Straits of Magellan. The gale in the narrow passage had been so fearful that the battleship was in danger of being dashed ashore against the great cliffs. The waves which were tossing the *Oregon* around had been so strong that the leadsmen could not man the chains. With dark coming on, the scene was terrifying. Down went the two anchors. Fortunately they gripped a rocky shelf and the battleship was saved.

The arrival of the *Oregon* at Key West was a proud day for the Navy and for America. A band on a warship welcomed her with "The Stars and Stripes Forever." The news of the *Oregon*'s arrival and a few days later the flash that Cervera's fleet was blockaded in Santiago Harbor let citizens on the East Coast breathe more easily.

On June 1, 1898, Admiral Sampson with the *Oregon* arrived off Santiago. But there was a problem. He could not risk his ships by steaming through the extremely narrow passage, paved with mines and lined with guns. The hurricane season was not far away, and when it arrived it would be difficult to maintain the blockade. For two weeks the Spanish ships had been in the harbor, and in this time they must have overhauled their machinery and boilers. It was not beyond probability that Cervera might, some dark night, bowl out of the channel and dash for the United States on a raid. Admiral Sampson pondered the best thing to do.

7   HOBSON AND THE *MERRIMAC*

IN THE first part of June, 1898, the admiral eyed Guantánamo Bay.

This magnificent sheet of water, almost landlocked, lies forty miles east of Santiago. It was deep enough to serve as an anchorage for the entire Navy. A base there would let ships take on coal no matter how fierce the gale.

When Sampson sent some of his fleet in with Marines to capture the place, the cruiser *Marblehead* was fortunate when a mine bumping against her plates failed to explode. Storming ashore, the Marines chased away the opposition, but the Spaniards, about three thousand strong, re-formed and battled the Marine outpost. For eight days the fight in the jungle raged. The marines terminated it by sending a combat patrol inland to destroy the well where the Spaniards drew their water. When the battleship *Texas* destroyed a fort at the water's edge, the Spaniards felt the odds were too great. They withdrew and the United States owned a splendid naval base.

During the skirmishes a Navy doctor and two Marines were killed. Naval Chaplain Jones wrote that the Marine colonel asked him to conduct the funeral. The bodies were wrapped in rubber blankets and placed in the graves. The Marines formed in line close by, and when the chaplain began, "Man that is born of woman..." a volley of bullets whistled over them from the jungle. Other Marines hustled up a fieldpiece and Colt automatic rifles. They could hardly make out the Spanish guerrillas because their bodies were painted green to blend with the heavy foliage. Chaplain Jones and the funeral escort stood their ground. He wrote that the officer in charge of the firing party said to his men, "Put regular cartridges in your rifles! We don't have blanks. Face toward the enemy and fire a salute over the dead. If you hit a Spaniard, so much the better."

Sampson's second decision, far more daring, was revealed when he was at Key West before he sailed with the *New York* and the *Oregon* for Santiago. He confided in young Mr. Hobson that he intended to sink the collier *Merrimac* in the channel leading into Santiago to cork up the Spanish fleet. The courteous and soft-spoken admiral asked Hobson how an iron ship could be scuttled quickly.

Instantly, Hobson said he was sure the scheme would work and begged that he be given command of the expedition. The old admiral believed in the young lieutenant with the clear-cut jaw and confident manner, but at the same time Sampson knew the excursion faced tremendous odds. It was obvious that as soon as the enemy discovered the expedition it would open fire with its coast-defense guns. The mines were also deadly obstacles. Hobson talked on, and the more he talked the more the admiral believed that he could accomplish the task. "Study it," the admiral told him.

When Sampson and the *New York* and the *Oregon* arrived

off Santiago, Hobson saw the *Merrimac,* and he regarded it with a new interest. Commodore Schley came on board the flagship and paid his respects to the admiral, who went over the hazardous plan with him.

The admiral gave Hobson the job, and the young officer immediately asked for volunteers. On each ship, when the captain assembled all hands and explained the idea, there was excitement. Almost all of the crew of three hundred on the *Texas* alone volunteered. Six hundred on the *Iowa* asked to go and almost as many volunteered on other ships. The captains eliminated men they could not spare, then Hobson was given the names of seven hundred men to choose from.

He decided that he needed seven men to man the collier. The volunteers he selected were: George Charette, of Lowell, Massachusetts; Osborne Deignan, of Sheart, Iowa; George F. Phillips, of Boston; Francis Kelly, of New York; Daniel Montague, of Wicklow, Ireland; John E. Murphy, also of Ireland; and Claus Clausen, of Denmark. The last two had become citizens of New York. Hobson himself was from Greensboro, Alabama.

On the *Iowa,* Seaman Paine offered Murphy $150 for his place, and Murphy turned him down.

There was a farewell conference in which Admiral Sampson went over the details once more with Lieutenant Hobson. The *Merrimac* was 333 feet long. The channel leading into the harbor varied in width from 350 to 450 feet. "It will be necessary," the admiral said to Hobson, "for you to bring her into the channel, swing her around until she is athwart it, hold her there, then sink her." Commodore Schley focused his telescope for Hobson and pointed out the forts the *Merrimac* and its suicide crew would have to face. The sprawling Morro Castle, on a high hill at the entrance, seemed especially forbidding. Its gun ports looked like dark splotches.

After the conference, Hobson secured a steam launch and

reconnoitered the harbor entrance from some distance out. He noticed a dark cave at the water's edge beneath the castle and decided he and his crew would rendezvous there after the *Merrimac* was sunk—while they waited to be rescued.

A large force helped Hobson prepare the *Merrimac* for her last voyage. She was stripped of extraneous equipment. Ten electric torpedoes, loaded with dynamite, were chained below the water line on her port side.

When his ship was ready, Hobson made sure each of his crew knew his job, and he drilled them to make doubly sure. He and his fearless sailors said good-bye to their friends and wrote "last letters" home. They prepared for the excursion by removing all their clothing except their shorts and undershirts. Each man strapped on a revolver. The only badge of rank Hobson wore was his officer's waist belt, which supported his pistol.

It was three in the morning on June 3 when the *Merrimac* steamed away from the U.S. fleet. The moon, an hour high, gave the warships a ghostly appearance. In the distance, below a dark cloud bank, loomed the headlands of Morro Point. Every man of the fleet who could do so watched the collier as she headed for the harbor's entrance.

Coxswain Clausen, at the wheel on the bridge of the *Merrimac*, took orders from Hobson, who stood close by. A shower of sparks burst from the collier's stack and fluttered out. The rather unwieldy ship smashed her way through the waves toward the spot that was to be her graveyard.

On the bridge of his flagship, Admiral Sampson watched the progress of the *Merrimac* through his telescope. Now the admiral had a new worry: the horizon to the east had become streaked with gray. He realized that the *Merrimac* would arrive at the harbor entrance at daybreak instead of in the dark. This would mean certain death for Hobson and his men and failure of the mission. Sampson sent a fast torpedo

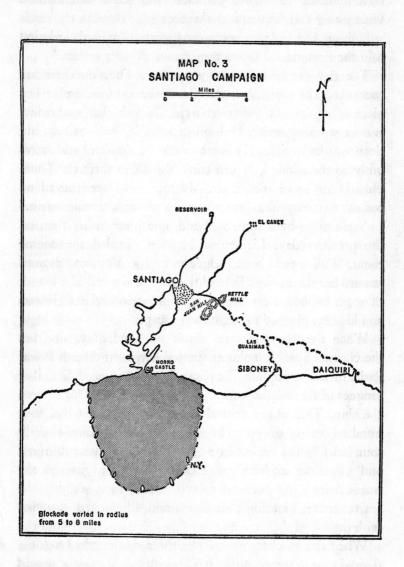

MAP No. 3
SANTIAGO CAMPAIGN
Miles
0   2   4   6

N

RESERVOIR

EL CANEY

SANTIAGO

KETTLE
HILL
SAN
JUAN HILL

LAS
GUASIMAS

MORRO
CASTLE   SIBONEY   DAIQUIRI

N.Y.

Blockade varied in radius
from 5 to 8 miles

boat to bring the *Merrimac* back, and the collier made a wide swing and returned to the fleet.

Hobson and his men were disappointed, until the admiral told the lieutenant, "Leave tomorrow, an hour earlier."

The day dragged for the volunteers. They checked and rechecked the torpedoes, the fuses, the engines, and every piece of equipment. After satisfying himself that everything was in working order, Hobson ordered his men to rest, but sleep was impossible. He went to the flagship and said nervously to the admiral, "I can carry this thing through. There must be no more recalls, sir. My men have been keyed up for over twenty-four hours and are under a terrific strain."

Again good-byes were said and, one hour earlier than on the previous day, Lieutenant Hobson signaled the engine room, "Full speed ahead." Once more the *Merrimac* plowed toward her destination. Behind the ship, at the end of a length of rope, bobbed a catamaran, a small raft on which Hobson and his men planned to make their escape.

When the *Merrimac* was about six hundred yards from the channel Spanish lookouts spotted her, even though it was dark. In a few seconds the shore batteries opened fire. Red tongues of flame lashed through the night. Projectiles pierced the ship. This was a critical time; the *Merrimac* had four hundred yards to go. The noise of the exploding shells sounded like the racket in a gigantic boiler factory. Mines and torpedoes exploded all about the doomed ship as she steamed into the harbor's mouth. Later, in describing the fearful scene, Fighting Bob Evans said, "It looked like Hell with the lid off."

When the blockade vessel was three shiplengths from the desired spot in the channel, two Spanish patrol boats appeared out of the darkness and shot away the *Merrimac*'s rudder.

Hobson signaled "Stop engines!" Both the lieutenant and Clausen wrestled with the steering wheel, but because of the broken rudder and the tide they could not bring the ship across the channel. She started to drift toward the Spanish fleet in the widest part of the harbor.

Machine-gun bullets banged through the ship's plates and smashed through the bridge. Hobson and Clausen ran just in time to save their lives. Hobson shouted to the men on deck, "Drop anchor!" The chains roared as the anchors plunged to the bottom. Crewmen worked to ignite the fuses, but enemy shells had severed the wires leading to the torpedoes. At Hobson's order the sea valves were opened and water water poured into the hold of the ship. The *Merrimac* lurched and began to list badly, sinking by the bow. Then she swayed over and plunged to starboard.

"Abandon ship!" Hobson screamed. He and his crew jumped over the side into the cold water and swam for their raft. The ship stood on its bow and disappeared beneath the waves. The swimmers fought for their lives as the suction of the sinking ship dragged them back and down. Fortunately, this struggle did not last long, because when the ship struck bottom the undertow stopped.

At the raft, Hobson and his men clung to its sides, their noses just above water. If they climbed aboard the catamaran they would be seen and killed, or captured.

More Spanish patrol boats appeared and searched the area. Finally, one of the patrol craft spotted the raft and hauled the shivering Americans out of the water. Admiral Cervera himself was aboard the Spanish boat. He had come to see what damage the *Merrimac* had done to navigation.

Lieutenant Hobson spoke Spanish to the admiral and pointed to his officer's pistol belt. Admiral Cervera put out his hand and welcomed the prisoners aboard. "*Valiente!*" he said. "Courageous!" Later, he sent a launch under a white flag to the American fleet to obtain the clothes of his captives, and he permitted Hobson to send Admiral Sampson a note. Hobson scrawled with pen and ink in shaky hand-writing:

Sir:

I have the honor to report that the Merrimac *is sunk in the channel. No loss, only bruises. We are prisoners of war, being well cared for.*

Very respectfully,
Richmond Pearson Hobson

The Americans were placed in cells in Morro Castle. While the place was extraordinarily gloomy, life brightened momentarily for the captives when Admiral Cervera, wearing full dress with a ceremonial sword, called on them.

The mission failed because the *Merrimac* did not completely block the channel, but the brave effort was hailed everywhere, even by the Spaniards. Admiral Sampson wrote a long dispatch to the Navy Department describing the deed and recommending Hobson and his crew for "a suitable award." When Hobson and his men were exchanged on July 6, there was great rejoicing in the Navy, in the Army, and everywhere in the United States.

Later, Hobson and his seven volunteers each received the Medal of Honor from President McKinley. In addition, Hobson was awarded the Specially Meritorious Medal and was promoted almost to the top of the list of commanders in the Navy.

Admiral Sampson organized his blockading ships so that the heavy guns of a battleship were always trained on the harbor entrance. A searchlight from one of the ships illuminated the narrow gap all night long. When the British naval attaché saw the searchlight, he called it "damned Yankee impudence." He was expressing in his British way his amazement at American initiative and unusual zeal.

Even though the Spanish fleet was not bottled securely, it seemed safe to Sampson to send a message to the Navy Department that the Army could land in Cuba. "We need ten thousand soldiers," he said. The war in Cuba had arrived at a point where the army and the navy had to team. The navy could not be expected to dislodge the Spaniards from their forts and positions about Santiago, nor to barge into the landlocked harbor when the Spanish fleet was inside, protected by belts of mines and forts.

The enlarged army was making frantic preparations so it could fight. It was anxious to get into action—the navy had so far reaped all the headlines.

Unpreparedness in the army when war arrived was nothing new. George Washington had a harrowing experience trying to conduct a war with a disorganized army. In his last message he warned, "For a people who are free and who mean to remain so, a well-organized and armed militia is their best security." His words had been forgotten, as they had been in the years before the Mexican and the Civil Wars. Once again the country was handicapped by the state of its Army. The men in ranks suffered, and in many cases were required to follow untrained, green leaders.

In the chaos of getting ready for a landing in Cuba, one of the most famous regiments in American history was formed. Its official name was the First Regiment of U.S. Cavalry Volunteers. It may not have been the most efficient regiment in the army's history, but no regiment attracted more headlines or surpassed it in eagerness and dash.

8   THE ROUGH RIDERS

SHORTLY after the United States declared war, Russell Alger acted to form three regiments of volunteer cavalry. His idea was that horsemen, well led, could strike hard and fast against the Cubans. Cavalry had played a valuable part in the Civil War in scouting, protecting wagon trains, finding the enemy, and fighting advance and rear-guard actions; and it had proved invaluable after the war against Indians and fighting renegades and bandits on the Mexican border.

But in forming the cavalry Alger did not consider the jungle trails of Cuba, where large bodies of horsemen would have a difficult time maneuvering. "Cavalry" sounded exciting. Telegrams went out to the governors of Indian Territory, Arizona, Oklahoma, and New Mexico, asking them to enroll men who could ride and shoot. Alger was anxious to locate the best leaders possible, and he offered the colonelcy of the First Regiment of U.S. Cavalry Volunteers to a man he knew was a leader, Theodore Roosevelt. Obviously Roosevelt was not going to sit the war out behind a desk in the Navy Department, in spite of advice from his friends that it was best for the country and his career if he did so.

Roosevelt thought that forming and joining a regiment of cavalry would be "bully," but he surprised the Secretary by turning down the eagles of a colonel. Roosevelt said that he had only three years of service in the New York National Guard, and that he knew a better man for the job, Leonard Wood. "I would like to serve under him as his lieutenant colonel," Roosevelt concluded.

Alger knew Wood well; in addition to his work at the White House, Wood was the Alger family physician. The Secretary thought his friend Roosevelt was making a mistake. "Wood can be the lieutenant colonel and do the work," Alger said. "You be the colonel."

Roosevelt declined. He knew that Dr. Wood had a far better military background. "T.R.," as the papers called him, told the Secretary that Wood was fearless, energetic, sober, dependable and friendly. He could have added "and very ambitious."

Wood's start in life was not calculated to carry him to high rank in the army. Having earned an MD degree at Harvard Medical School, he followed this with a short experience as an intern and physician. It seemed to him that opportunity and excitement lay in the West, so after taking and passing an examination for doctors, he signed for a tour with the army in Indian country as a contract surgeon, a hired physician.

He loved the West. When he had to ride horseback sixty or more miles to tend a sick cowboy he thought it an adventure. But there was one thing that kept Leonard Wood's ambition in bounds: in the army, except in an emergency, a doctor does not command soldiers.

It was difficult for both officers and men not to look to Wood for leadership. He was a bright and popular man, whom people naturally desired to please. Westerners delighted in telling stories about him. When the famous General Miles was in Los Angeles suffering from a broken leg he had received when a stagecoach overturned, he asked for the best doctor available. This was Wood, 580 miles away at Fort Huachuca, Arizona. When Wood received the summons to Los Angeles he would have ordinarily relished the ride, but he was tending a child who was seriously ill from typhoid fever. By staying at the fort Wood could save the child, so he turned down the general's request. With character like this, his reputation grew.

Not long after his arrival at Fort Huachuca, a wide search started for the cruel Indian chief, Geronimo. This was 1886. For fourteen months the army chased the Indian and his warriors thirteen hundred miles through the rough mountains of Arizona and New Mexico, through desolate country into Mexico and back. Leonard Wood reveled in the hardship.

Occasionally he met General Miles, who was in command of the campaign, and they became friends. In camp, when they had time, they boxed. One evening Wood smashed a rugged left into the general's face and the general collapsed. In a few moments Wood was treating him for a neck injury, a hurt that plagued Miles for a long time.

One of the great characters of the army, along with Miles and Wood, was Captain Henry Lawton. Lawton, an experienced soldier from Toledo, Ohio, and winner of the Medal of Honor against the Confederates, was directly in charge of the campaign to bring in Geronimo. He stood six feet four, and his tall flat-topped hat made him seem like a giant. A black handlebar moustache and his gruff talk made him appear distant, but Lawton was loved by almost every man serving under him. Once he barked at the contract surgeon, "Wood, what the hell are you doing out here, anyway?"

Dr. Wood told the truth. "Sir, I am trying to win an officer's commission."

During the campaign, Wood earned the Medal of Honor. He won it because he voluntarily carried dispatches through a region infested with hostile Indians, riding horseback seventy miles in one night and walking thirty miles the next day; and because he volunteered and commanded a detachment of infantry when it was without an officer. After Geronimo was captured, this unusual doctor was awarded the two bars of a captain in the army's Medical Corps.

Wood found an outlet for his energy back in civilization at Fort McPherson, Georgia, by playing guard on the Georgia Tech football team. Football was uncommonly rugged in the nineties. The guards were back of the line of scrimmage, where they could get a good start. Slugging was legal, there was no neutral zone, and an on-side kick to the flank made the game wide open. Ladies and girls were not supposed to attend football matches unless they wore veils.

After one Georgia-Georgia Tech game at Athens, there was a riot. Wood helped form the rear guard so his team and rooters could catch the train for Atlanta. He also played in San Francisco on the Olympic Club team with other college players, against the University of California.

In 1895, when Major Wood became the physician at the White House, his reputation placed him second to none in the Medical Corps. He was polished, virile and handsome. In off hours he and his friend Theodore Roosevelt liked to kick a football in Rock Creek Park.

The two friends kept each other informed about events in Cuba. Both thought that the United States should plunge into war and free the Cubans by defeating Butcher Weyler's Spaniards. When the *Maine* blew up, Wood promptly volunteered for combat. This was the man whom Roosevelt recommended as leader for the First Regiment of U.S. Cavalry Volunteers.

On Alger's recommendation, Dr. Wood became a colonel of the regiment and plunged into the work of securing necessary equipment. Roosevelt remained in the Navy Department for a while to wind up his affairs as assistant secretary.

Because Wood was acquainted with the problems the nation faced in readying its army, he was able to steal a march on other regiments. He knew there was a shortage of khaki cloth, that soldiers going to Cuba would have to wear blue woolen uniforms far more suitable to Alaska. Wood decided that the uniforms for his cavalry regiment would be khaki trousers, blue flannel shirt, and wide-brimmed campaign hat. With his energy and determination there was no stopping him. He got the clothing. Then from his office in Washington he worked to obtain horses, rations, forage for the animals, saddles, bridles, blankets, canteens, shoes, tents, and hundreds of other needed items. Because the heavy Civil War cavalry saber was out of date it would not be carried, but each soldier who wanted one would be given a machete, a long, wide-bladed knife, the type used to cut cane and brush in Cuba.

Some of the wealthy soldiers in the regiment bought two quick-firing guns and a Sims-Dudley dynamite gun. This weapon could lob five pounds of dynamite through the air at 600 feet per second. It was not accurate; a wind could cause the projectile to go far astray. Nevertheless they were happy with their long-barreled dynamite gun. It was said a weapon of this type had already been used effectively by Cuban guerrillas against the Spaniards. But most of all Wood's cavalrymen prized the new Krag-Jörgensen carbines their colonel had wangled for them. This weapon carried five bullets in the magazine and one in the chamber, and weighed only eight pounds. Other volunteer regiments were being issued antique .45-caliber single-shot Springfield rifles.

Before Roosevelt left Washington, preceding Wood to San Antonio, where the regiment was forming, he tried to ascertain the army's plans for the campaign. He wrote in his *An Autobiography*, "This was simple. The army had no plans."

Over twenty thousand young Americans tried to enlist in the regiment. The first requirement was that an applicant be able to ride and handle horses. Therefore many of the men were cowhands and ranchers from the West, but men applied from all over: from Yale, Harvard, Princeton, and other Eastern universities. Almost every type of athlete enrolled: baseball players, a star quarterback from Princeton, oarsmen, polo players, soccer players, boxers, track men, and so on. Scouts and hunters from the Great Plains volunteered. There was even a West Point cadet, on furlough from the Academy. Twenty regiments could have been formed. The initial quota was 708. Wood cautioned Roosevelt, "Don't enlist anyone whose belly is bigger than his chest."

When the regiment's strength was upped to one thousand, Roosevelt showed his tremendous pride in the new organization. "We can now promote deserving men," he said.

Newspaper reporters, attracted by the glamour of a regiment headed by two famous individuals, covered the assembly and stayed to write stories about the colonel and, especially, the lieutenant colonel. They dubbed the regiment "The Rough Riders."

Roosevelt was not certain at first that he liked the nickname, but signs appeared at the railroad station, THIS WAY TO THE CAMP OF THE ROUGH RIDERS. *Rough Rider* seemed to be an accolade, and Roosevelt soon reveled in the name. Some of the reporters sent dispatches about "Roosevelt's Rough Riders," but Wood was not upset. They were friends; he was proud of Teddy. And Wood wore the eagles.

At the railroad depot, a band welcomed newcomers by playing "There'll Be a Hot Time in the Old Town Tonight." Things looked gay until the Rough Riders appeared on the drill field; there their performance was ragged. At night, Lieutenant Colonel Roosevelt studied by lantern light in his tent to verse himself in the next day's drill schedule.

He wrote, "The tone of the officers' mess was very high," but he mingled with the men as soon as he left the table. He knew them and liked them. In his book *The Rough Riders*, his love for the regiment shines through in numerous places. He tells of the nicknames of some of the privates. "One unlucky and simpleminded cowpuncher, who had never been east of the Great Plains in his life, unwarily boasted that he had an aunt in New York, and ever afterward went by the name of 'Metropolitan Bill.' A huge redheaded Irishman was named 'Sheeny Solomon.' A young Jew who developed into one of the best fighters in the regiment accepted, with entire equanimity, the name of 'Pork-chop.' We had quite a number of professional gamblers who, I am bound to say, usually make good soldiers. One, who was almost abnormally quiet and gentle, was called 'Hell Roarer'; while another, his antithesis... was christened 'Prayerful James.' "

One of Roosevelt's heroes and a character in the regiment was Captain William "Buckey" O'Neill, a former sheriff and mayor of Prescott, Arizona. When the Rough Riders formed, Buckey O'Neill raised a company so fast that President McKinley sent him a telegram of thanks. On the day when O'Neill and his men left for San Antonio, the women of Prescott presented him with a silken flag, and the men also gave him a present. A judge made the presentation speech. "Captain O'Neill, we want to give you a mount. It is not full grown, but merely a Colt. We tell you that it bucks. Head it toward a Spaniard, and you can rest assured that one more Spaniard will bid his god-father, the devil, good morning." Then the judge handed Buckey a Colt pistol.

Captain O'Neill liked to say around the Rough Riders' camp, "I'm ready to take all the chances when we get to Cuba. Who would not gamble for a new star in the flag?" Evidently Buckey O'Neill had never heard of the Teller Amendment, and the Rough Rider regiment was a poor place to find out about it.

At first many of the Rough Riders did not see why they had to obey their officers, but Wood and Roosevelt convinced them that they could not win unless they had discipline. They realized that in Wood they had a leader with battlefield know-how. They loved Theodore Roosevelt, reciprocating his interest. His enthusiasm and spirit gave the regiment an *esprit*. And he did this in his own way.

Once after a hard drill session on the parade ground when the Texas sun scorched man and beast, Roosevelt bought a schooner of draft beer for every man in an entire squadron. Colonel Wood heard about it and summoned Lieutenant Colonel Roosevelt to his tent, where he explained that long-standing army custom decreed that officers did not drink with enlisted men. "The reason," Wood expounded, "is that you cannot socialize with men then expect them to jump when you give an order."

Roosevelt felt embarrassed. He apologized to the colonel and called himself "the damndest ass within ten miles of camp."

Leonard Wood explained the "rule" correctly, but if there was ever an officer in the United States Army who could violate this custom and still retain command and the respect of soldiers, that man was Theodore Roosevelt.

9 DEPARTURE OF THE CRUSADERS

WHEN Mr. Alger ordered cavalry to Chickamauga Park, Georgia, some of it departed from Fort Myer, Virginia. On April 21, 1898, Lieutenant Charles Dudley Rhodes wrote in his diary:

Three days have elapsed since we left Fort Meyer on the railroad. The farewells were sad and hard to make, as no one could tell how many might never return. On the Chesapeake and Ohio Railroad much patriotism was shown all along the way—flags, bands, fireworks and cheers, and in the small Southern towns the loyalty shown to the Flag was especially gratifying. There are many rumors about how soon we will be sent to Cuba....

A few days later in camp in Georgia he wrote:

The 24th Infantry Regiment [composed of Negro soldiers] and the 9th Cavalry received orders to go to Tampa to make a landing on Cuban soil. Many of our officers envy these regiments their opportunity.... All the officers are anxious to meet the Spaniards but deplore attempting active operations at this time of the year....

It *was* a bad time to go to Cuba because of the coming rainy season, but there was too much pressure on the Administration in Washington to resist. On May 10 the cavalry regiment to which Rhodes belonged was galvanized into action:

This morning at 8 o'clock a courier came galloping into camp. "Recall from drill" and "Assembly" were blown on the bugles, and we learned that we are to board the cars and head for Tampa. . . . In haste, written at the Depot.

There was wild confusion in Tampa. The little town of ten thousand on the west coast of Florida, about 240 miles from the southern tip of the state, was overrun with soldiers of the hastily improvised Expeditionary Force.

General William R. Shafter on the job was a resolute, common-sense, capable soldier who was gruff at times. This heavy-set man from Galesburg, Michigan, had established his reputation for courage at Fair Oaks in the Civil War. In the middle of that hard fight he was wounded but refused to be evacuated, and this won him the Medal of Honor. He was now sixty-three years old, stood five feet nine, and weighed over three hundred pounds. Physically, Shafter was not in good condition. His health had been worn thin by thirty-seven years of hard service, and he was burdened by his extra flesh, but soldiers liked to work under him because he knew his mind and seldom changed it. He was selected to lead the invasion because he was aggressive and had the ability to meet difficult situations. The chaos at Tampa was too great for any man to untangle, even a Shafter. It would have challenged a half-dozen wizards.

The War Department, swamped by the emergency, was rushing soldiers and supplies to Florida as fast as it could. There was but a single track between Tampa and the port from which the ships would sail, and freight cars loaded with supplies were backed up for miles.

In addition to his supply and logistic troubles, Shafter was flooded with instructions from Washington, such as:

... GO WITH YOUR FORCE TO CAPTURE GARRISON AT SANTIAGO AND ASSIST IN CAPTURING THE HARBOR AND FLEET. ...

It was not made clear how an army could assist in capturing a fleet.

The next day came another telegram from General Miles in Washington:

... ACCOMPLISH [THE MISSION] WITHOUT DELAY. CALL ON THE REBELS AND MAKE USE OF THEM AS YOU THINK ADVISABLE, ESPECIALLY AS SCOUTS AND GUIDES. YOU ARE CAUTIONED AGAINST PUTTING TOO MUCH CONFIDENCE IN ANY PERSONS OUTSIDE OF YOUR OWN TROOPS. YOU WILL TAKE EVERY PRECAUTION AGAINST AMBUSCADE OR SURPRISE, OR POSITIONS THAT HAVE BEEN MINED OR ARE COMMANDED BY THE SPANISH FORCES. ...

For an officer of General Shafter's experience such orders were an affront, but he did not get excited. The only people who ruffled him were newspaper correspondents. He disliked them intensely. At first his main goal was to try to organize a staff that could cope with the tangle at Tampa. However, the confusion was too far advanced.

Feverish work around the clock was under way at Port Tampa to place coal, water, a mountain of rations, forage, artillery, and ammunition on the transports. At the wharf there was one narrow place in which to work. In the absence of loading machinery, most of the supplies had to be carried aboard on the backs of stevedores who walked up and down steep gangplanks lugging their loads until they were exhausted. Carpenters worked long hours in the holds of the ships to build tiers of bunks for the soldiers and stalls for the animals.

Shafter's aide, the handsome and efficient Lieutenant John D. Miley of Illinois, wrote that everyone believed the transports could hold a total of 27,000 men, but that this was an error; only about 17,000 could go. The confusion mounted because parts of regiments had to be left behind. What loading plan existed collapsed. In the haste created by the Government in Washington, there was no time to make an orderly plan. Major Eben J. Swift, of the Seventh Illinois Volunteer Regiment, wrote, "The loading was chaotic. A battery of artillery was placed on one vessel and its ammunition on another."

There was tremendous disappointment in the regiments when it became known that parts of regiments would have to be left behind because of lack of space. This was especially true in certain cavalry regiments when the men were told they could not take their horses. It was hard to separate a man and his mount.

There was one officer, commanding a strange unit, who was determined to find space aboard the transports. This was the popular Second Lieutenant John H. Parker of Missouri, seven years out of West Point. He had a battery of four of the new Gatling guns. Parker was enthusiastic about the idea that the rapid-fire Gatlings could be wheeled to the front line in a battle and would help the infantry to move forward.

New ideas were unwelcome in many parts of the Army, but Colonel Arthur MacArthur (father of General Douglas MacArthur) listened, and so did General Shafter. These guns on wheels amounted to a cluster of rifle barrels bound together. When a crank was turned they revolved about a central axis, and bullets zipped out at a rate of nine hundred per minute. Many officers thought it foolish to give precious space aboard the transports to such an untried weapon, but Parker wangled permission and placed his Gatling guns aboard the transport *Cherokee.*

Although Mr. Alger would not let General Miles go to

Cuba, Miles, accompanied by his wife and two children, arrived in Tampa to see for himself how the loading was progressing and to do all he could to speed it up. He recorded his impressions:

Several of the volunteer regiments came here without arms, and some without blankets, tents, or camp equipage. The 32nd Michigan, which is among the best, came without arms. General Guy V. Henry reports that five regiments under his command are not fit to go into the field. There are over 300 cars loaded with war material about Tampa. . . . To illustrate the confusion, fifteen cars loaded with uniforms were side-tracked twenty-five miles away from Tampa, and remained there for weeks while the troops were suffering for clothing. Five thousand rifles, which were discovered yesterday, were needed by several regiments. . . . Ammunition [is] scattered through hundreds of cars on the side tracks of the railroads.

The army camps near Tampa were enough to cool the ardor of the most devoted volunteers. Some Regular Army units arrived on the sandy, pine-dotted area before the militia came and helped prepare the camps. However, when 44,000 men were dumped on the scene in the last two weeks of May, the Regular Army receptionists were overwhelmed. Sandy soil makes a bad camp ground, and here the sand reflected the heat of the sun. The militia regiments were not used to outdoor life nor to caring for themselves. Some of them had no cooks, utensils, or camp stoves, and were consequently unable to prepare meals when rations were issued in bulk. For soldiers in these regiments, existence became a matter of eating hardtack, cooking bacon over campfires, and boiling coffee in tin cans—the coffee beans were ground up by pounding them between rocks. Unsanitary conditions produced sickness. The doctors in the Army Medical Department were competent, but they lacked medicines and hospital supplies.

The War Department purchased a large supply of "canned

fresh beef," some of it from abroad, but by the time it was issued to the soldiers much of it was tainted. The rest was stringy
and almost tasteless. The soldiers called it "embalmed beef."
The War Department was staggering under its stupendous,
unaccustomed load.

In Tampa and nearby Lakeland, illicit characters of all kinds
arrived to fleece the soldiers. Fortunately many of the towns
near the camps did not sell beer or whiskey. A popular drink
was "the General Shafter Milk Shake," but there were so many
calls for it that the supply could not meet the demand.

On top of everything it was hot, and after dark armies of
mosquitoes attacked. The soldiers looked forward to one
thing: to get away from the camps.

When the Rough Riders arrived in their cooler uniforms,
they were the envy of the Regulars and militia, who were
sweating in heavy blue wool. Wood and Roosevelt, in tailor-
made uniforms, looked grand. It seemed unfair to many Regular officers that Leonard Wood, the President's doctor,
should be the colonel of a regiment, even though he had won
the Medal of Honor in the capture of Geronimo.

This did not worry Colonel Wood. The Rough Riders,
after their hard train trip from Texas with their horses, started
drilling all over again to perfect themselves. Like other cavalry
regiments, they were upset when they received the order that
there was no room for horses on the transports and that one
squadron of men could not be taken. One cavalry unit from
New Orleans was to take its horses, and other animals would
go along to transport supplies.

Five days after the Rough Riders arrived, the exciting order
came to cover the nine miles to Port Tampa and board ship.
The Rough Riders lost no time. A train of coal cars rolled by
and they stopped it, climbed in, and persuaded the engineer
to run them to the port. When they climbed out of the cars

at Port Tampa, men and uniforms were filthy, but they had arrived.

Wood and Roosevelt looked for men to guide them or to assign them to a ship, but they found nothing. Colonel Roosevelt was beside himself. He had feared all along that the war would be over before the Rough Riders arrived in Cuba, and now it looked as if they might be left in Florida. While the regiment waited, the two colonels hurried to find the quartermaster in charge. They located him and he pointed out a transport in the bay, the *Yucatan*. The colonels quickly discovered that the vessel had also been assigned to two other regiments.

To make sure that the Rough Riders got aboard, Colonel Wood commandeered a small boat and sailed out to the *Yucatan* while Roosevelt ran back to bring up the regiment. Wood talked the captain of the ship into bringing her to the dock so the Rough Riders could board her. They spent most of the day working to load their baggage and equipment. The scene below decks was shocking. The bunks, arranged in tiers, were expected to hold two men each. Roosevelt wrote later, "The men were packed like sardines."

The experiences of other regiments were similar.

In the meantime, on the evening of June 7, at the Tampa Bay Hotel where he had his headquarters, Shafter answered a summons to the telegraph office. President McKinley and Mr. Alger, in Washington, were at the other end of the wire. The operator in Tampa was replaced by a captain of the Signal Department, and after the telegraph had clicked off its message the captain handed the general a paper:

YOU WILL SAIL IMMEDIATELY, AS YOU ARE NEEDED AT DESTINATION.

R. A. ALGER
SECRETARY OF WAR

Shafter replied that he could sail in twelve hours, that the loading would continue all night, that it was impossible to get steam up before daybreak. President McKinley closed the telegraphic conference by telling General Shafter that word from Admiral Sampson at Santiago called for a quick arrival—before the Spanish strengthened the city's defenses.

At two in the morning General Shafter and his staff stepped aboard a special train at the hotel, rolled to the port, and boarded the steamer *Segurança*. The loading was still under way. After daybreak the ships lifted their anchors and headed toward the entrance of the bay. The thirty-two transports (coastal steamers) and auxiliary ships such as water tenders jockeyed into position. Bands played patriotic airs and the soldiers cheered.

Suddenly a launch cut through the water at top speed with a message for General Shafter: *The expedition was not to sail— by order of Mr. Alger.*

Shafter investigated and discovered that the Navy Department had requested a delay because of a report that a Spanish cruiser and a torpedo-boat destroyer were off the north coast of Cuba.

Because the port facilities were so small, the soldiers were kept aboard except for a few men on pass. It would have taken the army three days to disembark. Some of the horses were taken ashore for exercise. Life on the ships became monotonous, and the weather was hot. In the cramped quarters, men and animals suffered.

Lieutenant Rhodes, now aide-de-camp to General J. C. Breckinridge on board the *Segurança*, wrote to his wife:

We have not yet set sail for Cuban shores. But [the order] is expected to come today. We have 12,000 to 18,000 men, the pick of the Regular Army [with some volunteers].... Our destination is unknown but we think it will be Santiago. We have on board officers, soldiers, Cubans, war correspondents, attachés—a con-

glomeration. Twelve hundred men are crowded between decks.
... Three tiers of bunks under an eight foot ceiling. Only two
small air holes. One hundred and twenty men have no bunks at all
and have to sleep on the deck.

The attachés Lieutenant Rhodes referred to, eleven in number, were observers from foreign armies, present through the
courtesy of the United States. Each wore the uniform of his
country's Army. Shafter sat in the shade under a deck awning,
where he could enjoy the breeze, and received them one by
one.

Although very polite, each attaché sang the same tune:
Shafter's army was headed for disaster. To them, lack of training in the volunteer regiments, unsanitary camps, and the confusion at Port Tampa were omens of defeat. The French officer was particularly gloomy. He told the general that before
the French stormed ashore in 1895 at Madagascar they prac-
ticed the landing maneuver for a year. Shafter sat there, three
hundred pounds of no comment. Later he remembered what
the attachés had to say.

On June 13, 1898, word arrived from Mr. Alger that it was
safe to sail. Now it was discovered that about sixteen of the
transports needed water, and water tenders worked long hours
to supply them. The next day, at nine in the morning, the
flotilla sailed away on the first American crusade.

After a day's journey, when the convoy was near Dry Tor-
tugas off the southern tip of Florida, the battleship *Indiana* and
seven small warships joined it. The crusaders cheered the warships. Captain Henry Taylor, of the *Indiana*, boarded the
headquarters ship to pay his respects to General Shafter. The
leaders discussed two serious problems. The convoy was hob-
bled by the speed of the slowest ship, six knots per hour, and
the captains of the steamers were civilian masters. "It would
have been far better," Captain Taylor said to Shafter, "if we
had a naval officer on the bridge of each ship to keep the ship

in line and in its proper place." The naval captain proposed to the general that the convoy be divided into two parts. The fastest ships could speed ahead.

General Shafter thought over the suggestion and decided against it. He wanted to arrive with his army intact. Even then he knew there would be difficulties.

The 15,877 officers and men were more comfortable when the ships were under way because a brisk sea breeze lowered the temperature. Everyone felt better. They were at last headed for the beautiful island of Cuba—and the enemy.

Although most of the cavalry had been left behind (the cavalrymen who were along would fight on foot), there were a surprisingly large number of animals in hastily constructed stalls on the ships. This was before the day of the truck and automobile. Lieutenant Miley recorded in his careful way that for transport in Cuba there were aboard 390 pack mules, 946 mules trained to pull wagons, 571 government horses, and 381 horses belonging to officers. In the hold were 195 wagons and 7 ambulances. Two hundred and seventy-two teamsters and packers were in charge of the draft and pack animals.

On the *Segurança* were two Cuban doctors, experts in yellow fever. They could envision what would happen to an army heading in the summertime for the stinking city of Santiago. No one was sure how the horrible disease was transmitted, although Dr. Carlos Juan Finlay of Havana had suggested in 1881 that the disease was carried by the mosquito. But the distinguished doctor lacked the facilities to prove his theory, and people pooh-poohed his idea.

HAWAII | 12 AUGUST 1898

10 ISLANDS IN THE PACIFIC

In mid-June, 1898, President McKinley took time out from the worries of the war to consider Hawaii. Now that sugar from Cuba was cut off from the United States, sugar from Hawaii was increasingly important.

Five years before, many of the leading citizens, some of them missionaries who had brought Christianity to Hawaii, rebelled against the ruler of the islands, Queen Liliuokalani. They deposed her and applied to the United States for annexation. Two Presidents, Benjamin Harrison and Grover Cleveland, considered the idea with different reactions. Harrison liked it, Cleveland did not.

Americans were learning more about the "Paradise of the Pacific"—twenty beautiful islands, mountainous, yet with fertile plains and valleys. President McKinley was sure that the islands, with many useful industries and products, would become of even greater value as time went on.

However, there were serious problems. The people in Hawaii were concerned because Japan was sending more and more farmers and merchants, and because thousands of Japanese coolies were upsetting the labor situation. McKinley used his influence, and an annexation treaty with the provisional government of Hawaii was approved.

When many of the coolies were sent back to Japan, that country protested, and a Japanese cruiser appeared in Honolulu Harbor. The United States sent three warships. The difficulty was smoothed over—for the present—because of American interest in the war in Cuba.

Another territorial gain was accomplished in the same month.

Captain Henry Glass, commanding the U.S. cruiser *Charleston*, opened sealed orders in Hawaii. The word from Washington directed him to steam four thousand miles across the Pacific and to capture the island of Guam. Few Americans knew about Guam, although it produced rice, coffee, tobacco, pineapples, coconuts, copra, and lumber. This island, about twenty miles by seven, was the most populous in the Marianas group, a convenient stopping place for ships en route to the Philippines and the Far East. Henry Glass, who hailed from Kentucky and Illinois, readied his cruiser and sailed.

When he arrived at the west side of the island, he steamed slowly into the harbor of San Luis d'Apra and opened fire on a Spanish fort. Out sped a launch. A Spanish official asked permission to board the warship, and when he was on deck he said, "We apologize. We have no ammunition to return your salute."

"Salute?" Captain Glass roared. "Our countries are at war."

Glass sent for the Governor. The Governor sent word back that regulations did not permit him to board an enemy ship. Shortly the American flag was hauled to the top of the pole at Fort Santa Cruz, and the United States controlled Guam.

11   TO THE BEACH!

WHILE General Shafter was trying to load his transports for the invasion of Cuba, Admiral Sampson was also busy. His warships unleashed a series of bombardments against the Santiago forts, being careful not to hit Morro Castle because Hobson and his men had not yet been exchanged and were prisoners in its dungeon.

Large quantities of ammunition were expended, but there was little damage. The forts blasted back at the warships part of the time, with no effect. The bombardments did enliven the dreary blockade—monotonous days of hard work for the men of the fleet. In the almost insufferable heat the coal heavers at the furnaces suffered. Yet it was necessary to have steam ready in case Admiral Cervera and his ships dashed for freedom.

A break in the monotony was the arrival of the press boats. These ships, chartered by the newspapers, brought mail from home, and for some of the ships fresh eggs and fresh fruit. At night the "dynamite cruiser" *Vesuvius* steamed in close to the harbor entrance to fire aerial torpedoes at the forts from her pneumatic guns. The unbelievable detonations from the 500-pound shells sounded like a half-dozen thunderstorms rolled into one, and the display in the sky looked like a wild Fourth-of-July celebration.

A nervous cable from Washington to Admiral Sampson: ARE YOU SURE THAT THE SPANISH FLEET IS INSIDE THE HARBOR? caused the admiral to ask for a volunteer to go ashore, to slip through the Spanish lines and scout the harbor to make certain that the American fleet was not watching an empty nest.

The naval officer Sampson chose for the perilous mission, from the group who volunteered, was a man widely known in the fleet because of his cheerful personality and efficiency. This was Lieutenant Victor Blue of Laurinburg, North Carolina, eleven years out of the Naval Academy. He was selected because he had a reputation for sound judgment. Twelve days before he had been ashore trying to run ammunition and arms to the rebels.

Wearing his sword and full uniform, Blue boarded a launch and landed on a beach twenty miles west of the harbor. He thrashed around in the jungle for an hour, then ran across a sentinel. It was a dangerous moment. The sentinel listened instead of firing, then led Blue to the camp of General Jesus Rabi, a handsome full-blooded Carib Indian who commanded about five hundred Cuban rebels. General Rabi was noted for his strong character and grim humor. Once when he was asleep on the ground a Spanish deserter, who was in the camp, tried to kill him. The deserter's pistol misfired and Rabi woke up, arrested the would-be assassin, and charged him for "not keeping his pistol in good condition."

Rabi was delighted to help Blue. The Indian assigned a major as a guide, and Blue and the rebel started out. They traveled sixty miles on muleback over little-known jungle trails to an unguarded hill where Blue could view the harbor. He made notes on what he saw, as well as a sketch. Washington breathed easier about Shafter's expedition after Admiral Sampson cabled Blue's report on the enemy fleet.

A few days later Victor Blue volunteered to go ashore again, over the same route—this time to make accurate notes on the positions of the Spanish warships because the admiral was considering sweeping aside the mines and sending in fast destroyers for a torpedo attack. Blue's second report was also valuable, but the idea did not materialize. Blue was advanced five numbers on the promotion list for his extraordinary bravery, and received the Specially Meritorious Medal.

About the time Admiral Sampson sent Blue's report to Washington, Shafter's transports, in a loose formation five miles long, steamed into the Gulf. When they paralleled the north coast of Cuba they kept out of sight of land; only now and then the lookouts could see the tops of the mountain ranges, thin blue lines on the horizon. Some of the transports observed the Navy's request for a blackout, but others plowed along at night blazing with lights as if they were excursion boats on the Hudson River. When waves rocked the vessels many men, at sea for the first time, became sick. The smells below decks were foul. Measles broke out and sick soldiers were rowed to the hospital ship *Olivette*.

On the *Olivette* Harrie Hancock, war correspondent, wrote of a mishap and an investigation. Food on the ship was barely acceptable, and recognizing this when he was at Tampa the captain had a turkey placed aboard for himself. The cooks were baking it and delicious smells floated out of the galley. Down the voice tube from the captain's dining room came the words of the steward, "The cap'n says, send up his turkey."

In a moment the head cook shouted back, "For goodness sake, somebody stole the captain's turkey!"

The investigation produced nothing but complaints. The ship's officers did not find who took the turkey but the newspaper writers traced it down to the black gang at the furnaces. The correspondents kept the secret. Hancock wrote, "Our sympathy was with the stokers."

On Monday, June 20, the *Segurança*, followed by the rest of the transports, arrived off Santiago. It was a peculiar situation. The navy had expert knowledge of how to handle ships, the army very little, yet Admiral Sampson had no control over the thirty-two transports and auxiliary ships that were steaming about his blockade. The admiral was anxious to cooperate. He boarded the *Segurança* and greeted Shafter. Little thought had been given as to how the army was to get ashore. The Secretary of the Navy, in Washington, said it was not his responsibility to place soldiers on a beach. He warned, "No navy men should be worn out to put the army ashore." The army was unhappy because, in the voyage from Tampa, it had lost one of the lighters which would help in the landing. Sampson brushed aside the difficulty and said that he would furnish steam launches and as many lifeboats as he could to get the army ashore.

So that General Shafter could get an idea of the magnificent but rough terrain, the *Segurança* steamed slowly back and forth along the coast. The jungle-covered mountains behind the harbor were a backdrop for the Spanish forts and for Morro Castle on its awesome cliff.

The two leaders decided to confer with General García because he knew the beaches and trails as well as the Spanish dispositions. The Cuban general had attended a conference the day before on the *New York*, where he advised about landing places, but the roll of the ship made him seasick and he "conferred" from a horizontal position.

To see García in the jungle, the admiral summoned a steam launch. The 300-pound general was lowered over the side and with some difficulty was placed in the launch as it banged against the *Segurança*. When the party neared the shore, Cuban soldiers shouted with joy and ran into the surf to assist. General Shafter was helped to the back of a mule and the party started, accompanied by Cuban guards, for General Rabi's camp, where they would meet García.

The old rebel general, dressed in his best white uniform, welcomed his guests, and the conference started in Rabi's tent. It lasted one hour. It was Sampson's idea that if Shafter could land his men near the forts at the harbor's entrance and capture them, the Navy could move in with mine sweepers and then sail in and defeat Cervera's fleet.

General Shafter did not like the plan. First, it meant splitting his army; the Spaniards had forts on both sides of the entrance. He knew, too, that a landing operation is extremely difficult, and that an army is vulnerable until it has a firm foothold and until it has adequate supplies ashore. It would be hard to secure a beachhead—a foothold—under the enemy's coast-defense guns even if they were not the latest and best type. Next, his army was green, and the divisions had not worked together. Lastly, the admiral's plan meant that part of the army would have to scale a 240-foot bluff.

General García said that the best place to land was at Daiquiri. (*See* Map No. 3, page 69.) It had a good beach and fewer than three hundred enemy soldiers guarded it. There were about twelve thousand in and around Santiago. Shafter accepted García's idea.

At the end of the conference Cuban soldiers, ragged as they were, lined both sides of the trail back to the beach and stood at "present arms" to honor the two American military men. Both leaders and their staffs were impressed with the sincerity of the Cubans. They looked wretched, but they had given the Spaniards a hard time. García had placed his soldiers at Shafter's disposal, but the American wisely asked that they remain under Cuban control.

In telling of his plan at the conference, Shafter said that he wanted to arrive at Santiago as soon as possible and attack the Spaniards before they were reinforced, then the navy could enter the harbor and sink the Spanish fleet. He said the navy could assist the army in the landing by shelling a number of beaches so the Spanish would not know at which beach they would land. To García, the American general said that he would appreciate it if the Cubans would further confuse the Spanish by attacking thirty-five miles west of Santiago, and he also needed them to wipe out the Spanish at Daiquiri. It was a splendid landing plan.

Back on board the *Segurança*, the general wrote out his landing order for the next day; on the *New York* the admiral issued directions for the bombardment and for the steam launches and small boats to assist the army.

Rough weather prevented Shafter from calling a conference to go over the plan with his principal officers. However, by daybreak the senior leader on every ship but two knew what was expected of his men, as well as the order in which the divisions would storm ashore. There was considerable apprehension in every rank about the landing. Men wrote last letters home. General Lawton, probably the most experienced soldier in Shafter's force, would lead the first division ashore.

There was an old pier at Daiquiri that had been used in mining operations. Some boats might land there—provided the Spanish soldiers guarding the beach were overcome. The big questions were: How much fire would the Spanish put down along the beach and how high would the waves be?

Paragraph 3 of General Shafter's landing order of June 20, 1898, caused consternation among the reporters who were aboard the transports. Shafter was anxious that each precious space in the steam launches, in the small boats and on the lighter be occupied by a soldier who could fight. Paragraph 3 referred to the reporters. It said, "They will remain aboard ship until the landing is accomplished and until notified they can land."

This upset the writers. Most of them felt it their duty to go ashore with the first waves of troops and to report any fight that occurred.

Richard Harding Davis, the most famous war correspondent of his generation, thought the general entirely wrong. Davis, a vivid writer, had thousands of readers because he could recognize the picturesque as well as the news value of situations. He had already reported the Greek defeat in the Greco-Turkish War of 1896–97, Spanish cruelty in Cuba during the Ten Years' War, and had written a book on Cuba. He was brilliant, although some critics thought him at times overdramatic. Richard Harding Davis, a jaunty fellow, decided to explain to the general that he was wrong.

Twirling the slender bamboo cane he affected and wearing a neat jacket, crushed felt hat, wide-flowing black tie, and trousers thrust into hiking boots, Mr. Davis found General Shafter and gave him advice on how newsmen should be treated. Shafter listened, then said gruffly, "No reporters will go ashore until we have the beach under control."

"I am no ordinary reporter," Davis said with a touch of pride.

"I don't give a damn what you are," the general barked. "I'll treat all of you alike."

Shafter's abrupt treatment shocked Davis, and the general's attitude toward other newspapermen turned them against him. They made him a target whenever they had a chance and reported his actions in stories sprinkled with barbs. There is no doubt but that Shafter's place in history would have been brighter if he had been less abrupt with the war correspondents. His subordinates learned to like him. Beneath his rough exterior Shafter was kindly; he knew what he wanted and seldom changed his mind. Almost everyone, except the reporters, admired the way he refused to give in to his affliction: about one hundred pounds of extra flesh.

One reporter was not baffled by Shafter's order. This was Burr McIntosh of *Leslie's Weekly*. He had arrived in Tampa with a private letter to Shafter from the Secretary of War, asking the general to "extend all courtesies to Mr. McIntosh" and to permit him to sail on a transport to Cuba.

To deliver his letter, McIntosh boarded the *Segurança* in Port Tampa, knocked on the door of Shafter's stateroom, and handed the general the letter. Shafter merely glanced at it, tossed it aside and said, "Lieutenant Miley attends to that."

McIntosh had the courage to say, "I thought that a letter from Secretary Alger would cause the matter to be attended to."

General Shafter said, "I don't know anything about it. See my aide—Miley!"

Now aboard the *Mattewan* off Santiago, Burr McIntosh was anxious to leave the transport and go ashore with the first waves of soldiers, but Paragraph 3 of the order barred the way. He handed a sergeant his camera and asked him to take it ashore.

Bands on the transports were playing "The Star-Spangled Banner," "Yankee Doodle," and the hallmark tune of the war, "Hot Time." The powerful guns of the navy thundered at the beaches. Launches sped toward the different transports and lifeboats were lowered. McIntosh told later how, during the confusion, he managed to fall out of a "window on the quiet side of the ship." The shore at Daiquiri was only three-quarters of a mile away, so he started to swim.

A steam launch towing a boatload of infantrymen chugged

by. The coxswain of the launch slowed down so the soldiers could haul in the reporter. This was no easy job, because McIntosh weighed only fifty pounds less than Shafter.

"We don't have time to take you back to the ship," the coxswain shouted, "we are going to the beach!"

12 GENERAL AGAINST GENERAL

O N THE transport *Yucatán* Lieutenant Colonel Roosevelt
was beside himself because the landing was under way
and small boats had not yet called for the Rough Riders.
His former naval aide, Lieutenant Sharp, who had served
with him when he was Assistant Secretary of the Navy, sailed
by in command of the armed yatch *Vixen*. Roosevelt hailed
his friend and the Rough Riders landed ahead of schedule.

Roosevelt's unmilitary ways caused comment. He, the
Rough Riders, and Colonel Leonard Wood received reams
of publicity in the New York papers. Some news writers felt
that certain reporters "who would be sure to write things
up in the proper spirit" were favored by tips from the Rough
Riders and from Fighting Joe Wheeler, division commander
of the regiment. After Roosevelt engineered his early landing,
one reporter wrote, "Why is he permitted to defy those in
higher command?"

The infantrymen crowding the small boats were loaded down as foot soldiers always are in a landing. They carried blanket rolls (pup tent, woolen blanket and rubber blanket) over their left shoulders; haversacks crammed with food for three days; full canteens and a hundred rounds of ammunition per man. When the first rowboats, about thirty of them, rode the surf and grounded on the beach, the soldiers scrambled out and ran up the steep slope. Some boats landed at the pier.

Two lifeboats overturned in the thundering surf and threw out the occupants. The soldiers were carried beneath the waves, because of their heavy packs, and drowned. An expert swimmer from the extraordinary Rough Rider regiment volunteered to dive. He recovered the rifles, and later the bodies were found. Several of the small boats were dashed to pieces. Shortly the navy took the rest of the boats back for more men.

At the top of the beach the infantrymen walked through the primitive village of Daiquiri, with two of its houses on fire from the bombardment. Three wrecked locomotives stood near ruined machine shops. Not a Spaniard was in sight. A Cuban regiment of two hundred men strolled out of a coconut grove and formed for roll call. They wore straw hats, nondescript uniforms—most of them being in tatters— and shouldered almost every variety of rifle. From each belt hung a machete. Tom Hall, a Rough Rider, wrote, "The first sight of our Cuban allies is not reassuring ... most slovenly lot of men I have ever seen. . . . Apache Indians are dudes compared to them."

The Americans asked where the enemy was, and the Cuban colonel replied, "When the ships fired, about two hundred of them left for Siboney." He pointed along the shoreline toward a beach seven miles away.

The 22nd Regular Infantry's Color Guard unfurled the Stars and Stripes and the Americans removed their campaign hats and cheered. Scouts fanned out into the jungle to make sure that the landing continued to be unopposed. When the news that there were no Spaniards at Daiquiri was wigwagged to the ships, most of them moved closer. Some anchored between 400 and 500 yards from the beach.

The Spaniards faced a hard problem. About two and a half months prior to the landing Marshal Ramón Blanco y Erenas, who had replaced Weyler as Governor-General of Cuba, informed General Linares, who commanded the district around Santiago, that he had secret information from the United States that the Americans would attack Santiago. He did not disclose how he had obtained the information.

Linares had over 36,000 soldiers, in the eastern province of Cuba. He would have liked to have most of them in a central position so that when he was certain of the place where the Americans were landing he could move quickly with his army and cast them back into the sea. He knew that a force landing on a hostile beach is most vulnerable when it is first getting out of the boats, before it can organize ashore. However, Linares had the task of protecting Spanish families who were loyal to Spain. This also meant guarding property from the raids of the guerrillas. Also the roads to the beaches were poor, many of them just bridle paths or trails; an army could not move rapidly over them. So General Linares scattered his soldiers, some of them miles from Santiago. His men were brave enough and willing to fight, but they were poorly paid and often went hungry.

Two months before the landing Spanish engineers, with infantrymen as laborers, had fortified the land side of Santiago. Three lines of trenches were dug and carefully camouflaged; barbed wire was strung in front of the trenches;

and blockhouses were built at key points. General Linares was determined to make the Americans pay dearly.

There were problems, too, on the American side. Shafter needed horses and mules ashore—not just for officers to ride, but the mules would form pack trains to carry food and ammunition inland from the beaches. One volunteer regiment was already about to starve because its men had neglected to place three days' rations in their packs as Shafter had ordered. Animals were needed to pull artillery guns and the Gatlings.

To get the horses and mules ashore, they were blindfolded and pushed overboard. Men in the few rowboats that were not ferrying soldiers cruised about trying to remove the blindfolds and to herd the confused animals toward the beach. Buglers on the shore blew "Stable Call," "Assembly," and "Charge" in hopes the animals would stop thrashing about and would swim toward the beach. Most of them did, but about sixty of the poor creatures swam out to sea and were lost.

John Parker, on the transport *Cherokee*, found it necessary to continue to champion his Gatling guns. This lieutenant, who looked as powerful as his guns, was disturbed because they and his men had a low priority in the landing schedule, and because he thought the four Gatling guns and their ammunition, a load of sixty thousand pounds, were too heavy for rowboats. On board the ship was bridging material belonging to the engineers. Parker had an idea: he would borrow it and construct a huge raft to carry his Gatlings ashore. The engineers objected. They were afraid the pontons would be smashed. At this moment General Shafter had a message wigwagged to the *Cherokee: "Have the Gatlings been landed?"*

Parker flagged back the answer: *"No."*

Shafter's personal interest in the Gatlings caused the engineers to reconsider their answer to Parker, but just then Brigadier General S. S. Sumner, prominent cavalry officer helping with supplies, ordered the *Cherokee* out to sea so that a supply ship could move to the pier. In an argument with the general and the engineers, Parker said, "What the hell are these boats made for, if they're not to be used and smashed up?" This irritated the general and the ship headed for sea.

Parker did not quit. He caused a message to be wigwagged to General Shafter that he was unable to carry out orders to land the Gatlings. Shafter resolved the situation by ordering that a lighter, used for freight, be loaned to the determined lieutenant, and soon Shafter himself arrived in a launch to be sure that Lieutenant Parker, his thirty-two men, and his powerful Gatling guns were put ashore. On the beach John Henry Parker of Missouri corraled eight Missouri mules for his battery.

To move the army on to Santiago so it could help the navy, and to get there before the Spaniards could bring in soldiers from inland positions, Shafter ordered soldiers landed at Siboney as soon as he found the enemy had left there. It was seven miles closer to the city.

Things were moving very well, although two transports, the *Saratoga* and the *City of Washington*, carrying a total of two thousand soldiers, could not be found. The general asked Admiral Sampson to round them up and have them land their soldiers at Siboney. On the whole Shafter was happy. Meeting no enemy at Daiquiri was especially pleasing.

But not everyone was pleased with the general. Richard Harding Davis' reports were overly critical. They also disclosed that Davis knew little about landing operations. Lieutenant Colonel Roosevelt wrote a friend condemning General Shafter because he "is not yet ashore." Shafter was in his proper place on his headquarters ship, where he could direct, but Roosevelt evidently thought he should be in the front ranks, as leaders often were when they fought Indians before the Civil War. On June 22, the day of the landing, Lieutenant Rhodes found time to write his wife from Daiquiri:

General Breckinridge [Rhodes was his aide] is embarrassed. He ranks Shafter as a major general. Nevertheless Shafter commands the expedition, and he is gruff and mean to General Breckinridge and doesn't show him any courtesies to speak of. Shafter is an old pig anyhow, but he is said to be a fighter and that is what we want for these bloody Spanish.

Later, Rhodes had a better opinion of the senior general.

13   FIGHT ON THE TRAIL

GENERAL SHAFTER was anxious to reach Santiago, but he was even more anxious not to go off half-cocked. He wanted his army well organized so as to increase its chance of defeating the enemy.

The little beach town of Siboney was now his base of operations. To place a mountain of supplies ashore, his men labored long hours. He had given his best soldier, Henry Lawton, who had risen from private to major general—the same officer who had been decorated for bravery before Atlanta in the Civil War and who had captured Geronimo—directions to protect Siboney "until we are ready to march against the enemy."

Lawton posted soldiers two miles up the jungle trail toward Las Guasimas (*see* Map No. 3, page 69) and spread his men out as a fan to protect the landing area.

Up the trail on a big horse trotted Fighting Joe Wheeler, looking something like an ancient, wizened jockey. Wheeler, now a major general instead of a Member of Congress, had seen numerous actions since he fought Indians on the frontier as a second lieutenant of Mounted Rifles. In the Civil War he had been wounded three times and had had sixteen horses shot beneath him. There was never a question of his bravery or enthusiasm for a fight, but at times the old Confederate acted as if he were a scout instead of a major general whose task it was to direct and to coordinate a battle. He was sixty-two and looked ninety because of his white whiskers and beard. Perhaps some of the pompousness he displayed in the War Between the States when he referred to himself in the third person as the "War Child"—"The War Child rides to-night"—was gone. In its place was exceptional confidence. In the Civil War his cavalrymen were criticized for lack of discipline; in Cuba in 1898 he acted as if he were trying to nail down fame.

Wheeler had landed at Daiquiri in advance of his men. When the Rough Riders arrived he ordered Colonel Leonard Wood to raise the Rough Riders' flag over a deserted enemy blockhouse. "There were shrill whistles from the entire fleet," Wheeler wrote.

On the trail north of the beach at Siboney the two generals, Lawton and Wheeler, were at cross purposes. Lawton, in command of the beachhead outpost, was amazed when Wheeler said he had 950 men, most of them Rough Riders, marching up the path and that he was going to lead them against the enemy. This was not in consonance with Lawton's instructions, but Wheeler was "the ranking officer ashore," so Lawton gave way. The story goes that he asked the little general why he was barging through the outpost, and when Wheeler could give no satisfactory answer, Lawton said, "I was given command of the advance, and I propose to keep it even if I have to put out a guard to make sure you and your men stay back. This isn't a political campaign!" But Lawton let them pass through the outpost.

Into the enemy country in the misty daylight of June 24, 1898, headed the Rough Riders. Before the dismounted cavalrymen left, Colonel Wood ordered troop commander Captain Capron to send forward five men as a point up the trail. Two Cuban scouts walked ahead of the point. In command of this post of danger was young, rawboned Sergeant Hamilton Fish. His grandfather, who was Secretary of State for President Grant, had helped avert an earlier war with Cuba. Captain Capron's troop was chosen to lead out and to find the enemy because he was efficient and dependable. Teddy Roosevelt described this tall, lithe athlete as "on the whole, the best soldier in the Rough Riders." Capron's father was also in Cuba as a captain commanding a battery of field artillery.

The tropical forest was gorgeous. Sunlight streaming through the trees made the place seem like a cathedral. Thick underbrush, royal poinciana trees dotted with scarlet flowers, thickets of white orchids, lime trees, and "Spanish bayonet" —a swordlike plant with narrow leaves three feet long that can cut like a knife—bordered the way.

The Rough Riders were tired. The air was humid and oppressive. The night before the Rough Riders had made a forced march from Daiquiri to Siboney, so Wheeler would have them on hand to strike out. In the last twenty-four hours they had had only about three hours sleep. The majority of them were cowboys and ranchers who were not used to walking, and their legs were cramped by the restriction of two weeks on the transports. At rest stops every variety of bugs attacked. Hiking on the slimy jungle trail itself was difficult. The mud, in some places a foot deep, sopped their shoes and seemed to be trying to hold them back. Some men cast their equipment into the brush to lighten their loads. Others cursed.

"Pass the word back, 'Silence in ranks!'" Colonel Wood said to his adjutant, and the word was passed back.

In a few minutes Roosevelt hurried up to Wood, saluted, and said, "Sir, the men are tired from being cooped up on ship. The doctor says the pace is too fast. About fifty have fallen out from exhaustion."

Wood acted as if he were back on the trail after Geronimo. "I have no time for that now," he snapped. "We are near the enemy."

About three miles beyond Siboney, toward Santiago, the marchers came across the dead body of a Spanish soldier in the trail. Cuban scouts had previously informed Wood that when he saw this body he would be about five hundred yards from the enemy's earthworks. Ahead there was a tiny clearing, on the right a jungle-covered hill. Open country was on the left. Just ahead bubbled a creek.

"We are close to Las Guasimas," a Cuban guide said to Captain Capron.

A volley of bullets ripped into the men as the point of the advance guard waded the creek. The foliage was thick, and because the Spaniards were using smokeless powder no one could see where the bullets came from. Sergeant Ham Fish fell forward, a bullet through his heart. Close by a private slumped into a sitting position, mortally wounded. Two more privates were hit. Captain Capron sent a verbal message back, "I think we have discovered a Spanish outpost." Then he was shot dead. On the other side of the creek Color Sergeant Albert Wright, carrying the Stars and Stripes, stood his ground. Three bullets whipped through the flag.

Lieutenant Colonel Roosevelt, a lieutenant and ten troopers rushed up and took cover in the knee-high grass, but they could not locate the enemy. Spanish bullets whipped over them. Roosevelt crawled farther, took a wounded man's rifle, and shot at locations where he thought the enemy might be hidden.

In a few minutes, back directing men, Roosevelt explained the situation to his friend Richard Harding Davis. Davis borrowed Roosevelt's field glasses and located the enemy on the hillside.

Some of the wounded men were screaming. Bullets hummed above them, an evil cover. Lieutenant James Robb Church, of Chicago, former "rusher" on the Princeton football team, now assistant surgeon of the Rough Riders, heard the cries of the wounded. This star athlete dashed into the little area, disregarding the bullets, picked up a wounded man, cradled him in his powerful arms, and ran with him down the trail to safety. Dr. Church risked his life three more times to carry out seriously wounded men, lugging them either in his arms or on his back. Fortunately this brave man was not struck by a bullet. His wounded received first aid at a temporary medical station further down the trail.

Eight years later, when Theodore Roosevelt was President, he signed an Executive Order directing that ceremonies at which the Medal of Honor is awarded "will be formal and impressive. . . . When practicable [the individual receiving the Medal] will be ordered to Washington, D.C., and the presentation will be made by the President. . . ." It gave Roosevelt extreme pleasure to bring James Church to the White House to be the first to receive the Medal under the terms of the new order.

Shortly after Church performed his valiant and unselfish deed, Fighting Joe Wheeler rode up the trail. He dismounted and examined the situation. He was as anxious as Teddy Roosevelt to fight—personally. In a little while it was obvious that the Rough Riders were up against a strong position and superior numbers. They needed help.

Wheeler sent a messenger riding back to General Lawton with a note: "Have encountered a bigger force than I anticipated." The message asked Lawton for help. Henry Lawton responded by sending two regiments of Regulars.

When the reinforcements arrived, Wheeler sent Colonel Wood and the Rough Riders to attack the Spanish from the left. Then Major General Wheeler led a combat patrol against the enemy. With him was Brigadier General Sam Young, who had been a private in the Civil War. They had with them about 130 Regulars, half of them well-trained Negro soldiers from the Tenth Cavalry—fighting on foot. Wheeler's little force attacked the Spanish from the right. The rest of the Regulars squirmed through the underbrush and poured accurate fire on the Spaniards.

After an hour's hard fight, the enemy left his entrenchments in a hurry. Fighting Joe Wheeler jerked off his campaign hat and yelled at his soldiers, "We've got the damned Yankees on the run!" That night Joe Wheeler's lapse was told over and over and acted out around the campfires. Former Confederate soldiers, now serving the flag of the United States, particularly enjoyed this story on Wheeler.

Later in the week it was discovered that, against the 964 Americans in the fight at Las Guasimas, the Spanish who retreated by order of General Linares had 1,500 men.

Linares had made a bad mistake. Not only did he have a splendid position blocking the road to Santiago, but he had another two thousand soldiers not far away that could have helped. Had he been more determined he could have gained time, enabling men to be brought to Santiago from other parts of Cuba. His strong position could have cost many American lives.

When the enemy retreated, Wheeler reported to Shafter that the Rough Riders were too exhausted to pursue.

Back on the trail, Roosevelt had the Rough Riders build

litters by cutting poles and using pup tents. The wounded were carried to the rear for treatment. A Spanish combat patrol slipped through the jungle and fired at some of the men on the litters, even though they were protected by Red Cross flags. This infuriated the Americans.

When the enemy patrol had been overcome, Trooper George Roland, of Deming, New Mexico, exhibited the spirit of the Rough Riders when he was told that his wound was so serious he would be shipped back to the United States. That night Roland managed to get out of the field hospital and reported back for duty with his pack and rifle. Roosevelt retained this courageous man.

One of the wounded hummed "My Country 'Tis of Thee," as he was carried down the path. The Rough Riders picked up the tune and soon the jungle rang with the hymn. Then came the sad task of burying the dead. Already vultures, "the scavengers of the tropics," were circling overhead. Some of the big black birds landed and tore the eyes from the dead. When the Marines had battled at Guantánamo, Admiral Sampson was upset because a report reached him that the Spanish had mutilated Americans killed in action. Later it was discovered that the foul work had been accomplished by vultures.

Sixteen Americans gave up their lives at Las Guasimas and twenty-four were wounded.

After the fight Wheeler wrote of it in glowing terms. Shafter was delighted over the offensive spirit, although he knew that Wheeler in pushing up the trail had further complicated the supply problem. He gave Wheeler orders not to go farther toward Santiago until more supplies were ashore.

At this moment Colonel Wood took Brigadier General Young's place because Young was ill with fever. This put the unusual Lieutenant Colonel Roosevelt in command of the Rough Riders.

Downpours of rain drenched the soldiers. Many men who had cast away their packs lost them when eight hundred Cubans hiked up the trail during the fight. Back on the beach, plunderers looted officers' baggage as it came ashore. Food was needed. Instead of delegating authority to a trustworthy captain to go back for supplies, Colonel Roosevelt rounded up all the mules he could and personally led a pack train back and forth to the beach to bring up food. He also bought food from his own pocket—beans and canned tomatoes—for his Rough Riders.

When the order came to form another outpost, the tired soldiers dragged themselves through jungle vines, up hills and down glades. Then there was trouble. Soon after dark, jittery sentinels in the outpost cut loose with their rifles. They thought the Spanish had come back in a night attack. The underbrush crackled as if a thousand Spaniards were crawling in it. Soldiers in the main camps along the trail were awakened and loaded their weapons. Bullets whined in every direction. Shortly it was discovered that hideous land crabs, tremendous ones with thick shells, had crawled from their holes and were out for food. It was their rustling in the undergrowth that had frightened the sentinels.

Charles Johnson Post, artist-writer, a soldier in one of the regiments, wrote in his interesting story, *The Little War of Private Post*, that when the firing started at the outpost his captain, far back on the trail, hiked rapidly to the scene of the firing. Shots clipped branches over his head and banged into nearby trees.

"Don't shoot!" the captain shouted.

"Halt! Who's there?" challenged a terrified sentry.

"I'm the captain," was the answer. "Don't shoot! Damn it, don't you know my voice?"

Promiscuous firing went on all night long. Sleep was almost

impossible with the scavenger crabs crawling over the ground and the outpost blazing away.

The day after the fight on the trail Lieutenant Rhodes summed up the fight in a letter to his mother:

> You probably read about the fight at Las Guasimas. . . . We met the litter bearers bringing in the wounded. We lost about 17 killed and 63 wounded; the Spanish, 40 killed. . . . I saw the horrors of war in the dead and dying and the subsequent interment.
>
> I don't like being aide-de-camp. The general is like a child in many ways and aides seem to be expected to do "the dancing attendance." No one knows a great man's weakness and foibles as well as his valet and if he is a general this applies to his aides.

Shafter, who had remained aboard ship until most of the supplies had been placed ashore, rode up the trail to inspect. His weakness was apparent. The heat and the exertion of riding horseback exhausted him. To move he had hoisted his huge weight onto a buckboard—which now sagged badly in the middle. Driving up the rough road to the front, he listened to reports from the officers, then ordered them to have their soldiers do what they could to improve the road. It was hard to widen or to drain because it was a narrow sunken road. When it rained this wretched trail became a gutter.

Shafter had much on his mind, and in a few days, after his reports had been digested in Washington and the stories of the reporters were in United States papers, he received a cable from Secretary of War Alger asking if the body of Hamilton Fish had been embalmed. HOW CAN HEAVY CASKETS BE GOT TO THE PLACE OF BURIAL, Alger inquired, IF THE PARENTS SHOULD WISH TO REMOVE THE BODIES?

Shafter felt ill, not because of such cables but because of his condition and the heat, but he did not lose sight of the critical problem: supply. He had been handicapped by the slipshod manner in which the transports had been loaded in Florida and by the lack of small boats and piers in Cuba. He knew that some commanding officers had not carried out his orders that each man going ashore carry three days' rations and that some packs had been discarded. It was obvious that food was being consumed. He pushed as hard as he could to build up supplies near the beaches for fear that a hurricane would drive his ships away.

Food was required up the trail. At first the general thought that pack trains could haul it, but many of the packers became ill. This was serious because it takes experience to lash a diamond hitch over a bundle of supplies on a mule's back. When amateur packers tried to tie on loads, the mules bucked them off and supplies were distributed along the path. The general ordered his hard-working quartermaster, Lieutenant Colonel Humphrey, to bring wagons ashore. Humphrey caused sixty-eight of them to be unloaded, but when they were employed on the uneven, half-flooded trail, many of them broke down. The general finally parceled out both mules and wagons to the various divisions so ammunition and rations could go forward. He installed a traffic-control system to permit the narrow trail to handle the wagons, each drawn by six husky mules.

The work of Major Frank Greene aided Shafter immensely, for Greene installed a telephone system so the general could talk to his division commanders. The cable connection at Guantánamo was restored, so the general had communication with Washington not too far away. This was not always an advantage.

There was much work to be done ashore in addition to fighting, yet the morale of Shafter's army so far was excellent. The soldiers seemed to relish the hardships in the jungle. The series of frustrations since the *Maine* blew up— life in the wretched camps, existence aboard the "prison hulks" as the men called the transports—had not daunted their spirit. In the forest at sunset they renewed their faith in the mission when regimental bands played "The Star-Spangled Banner."

The crusaders of '98 looked to Shafter to signal them to march on Santiago. Cuban scouts spread the word that eight thousand Spanish soldiers were fifty-four miles northwest of the city and were hiking toward it. They had with them a large herd of beef cattle and other supplies. The crusaders girded themselves for a showdown fight.

14   EL CANEY

HowevER, there was a brief time for rest. Many of the soldiers went on hunts for tropical fruits: mangoes, coconuts, scrub bananas and more limes. A private yatch belonging to the newspaper magnate Hearst anchored off Siboney. With his compliments, he sent ashore a four-page newspaper he had printed aboard the yatch.

Now Cuban scouts brought Shafter reports on the Spaniards, but he was suspicious. He wanted information that was checked by his own people.

Richard Harding Davis jumped at this. In one of his barbs at the general, he wrote, "The only reconnaissance the officers were permitted to make was to walk out a mile and a half beyond the outposts." Davis continued, "There were in the Rough Riders alone several hundred men who for years had been engaged in just that work, scouting and trailing." Davis *did* mention that Brigadier General Adna R. Chaffee had acquainted himself with the country.

Actually, General Shafter sent George Derby, twenty-two

years out of West Point, a trained engineer, to explore. On this dangerous mission, which took him close to enemy positions, Lieutenant Colonel Derby took along six young officers. His party felt its way forward, made sketches and estimates, and mapped the enemy earthworks and important trails. For his efficient and hazardous work Derby was given a Silver Star Citation. Two generals in addition to Chaffee —Wheeler and Lawton—and other leaders also scouted forward. Wheeler was not well, but with his audacity there was no keeping him back. Just before the advance started, Shafter himself, with his two aides, scouted ahead so he could visualize the key enemy positions: El Caney and San Juan Heights. Cuban pickets stopped them two hundred yards short of the Spanish lines.

When all available information was plotted on his map, Shafter made his plan.

The Spanish at El Caney posed a difficult problem for him. Reports varied on the strength of the El Caney garrison. Some merely said it was "strong." General García said, "It has fifteen hundred Spaniards." Some of Shafter's scouts reported the number as "five hundred with about one hundred others in the town who might fight." There was no way for Shafter to be sure of the size of the enemy forces in El Caney.

He studied the sketches made by Derby. At El Caney there were four blockhouses, barbed wire, a stone church fitted with loopholes, rifle pits, and trenches. You could go from one blockhouse to another in the deep trenches and not be seen. Open country sloping up to the town and the fortifications made it a strong position. In addition—and very important—was that the Cubans said the Spanish leader there, Brigadier General Vara de Rey, was *mucho hombre*.

The city of Santiago was protected by an even greater network of blockhouses, stone forts, trenches, and barbed wire. General Shafter wanted to move quickly in an attack against

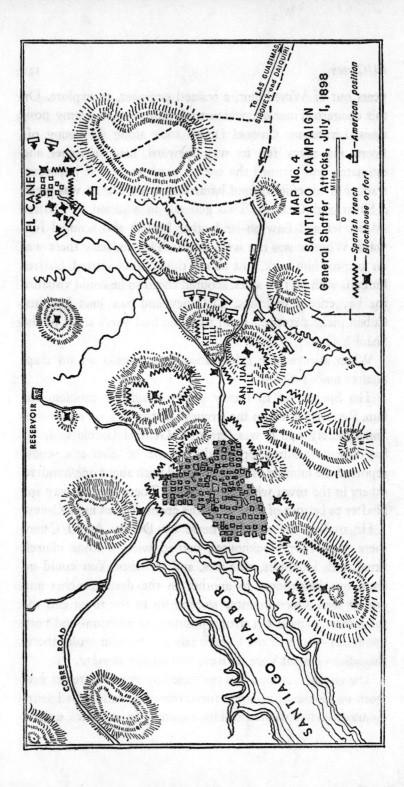

MAP No. 4

SANTIAGO CAMPAIGN, July 1, 1898

General Shafter Attacks

Miles

WWWW — Spanish trench

— American position

▲ — Blockhouse or fort

TO LAS GUASIMAS,
SIBONEY and DAIQUIRI

EL CANEY

RESERVOIR

KETTLE HILL

SAN JUAN HILL

San Juan River

COBRE ROAD

SANTIAGO HARBOR

Santiago, but what was he going to do about the garrison at El Caney? If he left it alone, General Vara might sweep down the two and a half miles and strike the American army in the flank, catching it on the narrow trails. Vara knew the ground.

Shafter discussed the problem with Lawton. Lawton said he expected his division could capture El Caney in two hours. "That's fine," Shafter said. "You take it. Then come down to those hills near San Juan and help us capture them. We'll wait on you."

General Shafter was concerned over casualties that could occur in his army. He thought that by capturing El Caney first, fewer men would be killed than if he were confronted later by the men from El Caney.

Shafter sent word to García and his three thousand Cubans, who were in the jungles three miles north of the city, to please block the Cobre Road so Spanish reinforcements could not arrive. García vowed that not a Spaniard would pass. Shafter's plan was good. If it succeeded, the water supply for the city, the reservoir to the north, would be controlled by the Americans. There was only one factor that was not considered: the courage of General Joaquín Vara de Rey.

On June 30, the Americans started moving for the next day's attack. They would bivouac near the positions from which they would start the fight. Lawton and his division swung off to the north for El Caney. This time the Rough Riders were not in the advance. They stepped aside, off the muddy trail at Las Guasimas, and sat down, waiting for orders as thousands of men marched by. It seemed to Teddy Roosevelt that the time for the Rough Riders to move toward Santiago would never arrive.

On a ridge facing El Caney American field artillery, drawn by horses, swept into position and unlimbered. While the animals were being led to the rear the gun crews got ready to fire. It was 6:30 A.M. on July 1, 1898. The American artillery blasted away, but the mile-and-a-half range was too great for the shells to do much damage. Lawton's infantry moved to the attack. It was stopped by well-aimed fire from the trenches and blockhouses.

The Second Massachusetts Infantry, attacking straight up the road toward the stone fort, was at a disadvantage: its black powder showed the enemy where every rifleman was. The black powder gave the same effect as if each Massachusetts man had a large sign reading, "I am here!" Modern Mauser rifles in the hands of the Spaniards forced the handicapped Second Massachusetts Regiment out of the firing line. The "two-hour" attack ran into the afternoon. Shafter sent a brigade to help Lawton.

Inside the hard-pressed defenses Brigadier General Vara, his two sons fighting at his side, was wounded in both legs. He was somewhat like a determined quarterback at the end of a losing football game who refuses to admit defeat. Vara's men were suffering, but they were punishing almost half of Shafter's army.

The heat and the excitement of battle tired the Americans. Hundreds of them were wounded. The Seventh U.S. Infantry, trying to circle a blockhouse and its trenches on the northeast side of the Spanish position, had thirty-three men killed and ninety-nine wounded.

American heroism of the most unselfish type was on display: nine soldiers were later awarded the Medal of Honor for "gallantly assisting in the rescue of the wounded from the front lines and under heavy fire from the enemy." *

*These men were: George Berg of Wayne County, Illinois; Oscar Brookin of Byron, Wisconsin; Ulysses Buzzard of Armstrong, Pennsylvania; John De Swan of Philadelphia, Pennsylvania; Thomas Graves of Milton, Indiana; Benjamin Hardaway of Benleyville, Kentucky; Norman Ressler of Dalmatia, Pennsylvania; Charles Roberts of Fort D. A. Russell, Wyoming; and Bruno Wende of Canton, Ohio.

The Americans were gradually tightening the semicircle about El Caney, but the fight was far from won. Shafter, who realized that the battle could be pursued in a smarter way, wrote a message:

Lawton: I would not bother with the little blockhouses. They can't harm us....

Shafter was right. If the blockhouses were bypassed, with maybe a hundred men being left to surround them, their defenders would eventually be starved out. But the message would have been more helpful if it had been sent earlier.

Late in the battle, the American artillerymen hitched up their horses and dashed forward to new positions closer to the enemy, where their guns would be more effective.

At five in the afternoon the Twelfth U.S. Infantry, tired, out of water, and under fire from the stone fort across the valley, increased its fire from a jungle hillside covered with "Spanish bayonet." Finally the Twelfth was given the order to charge. Its men raced downhill and then up the opposite hill to the fort. They poured through breaches in the stone walls carved by the artillery. In the hand-to-hand fighting, Private Joseph Abele sprang to the bastions of the fort and waved the American flag, and the valiant Spaniards, almost out of ammunition, surrendered. General Vara, the mainspring of the defenses, was dead.

Down fluttered the red-and-yellow flag of Spain, one of the best-known flags in the world. El Caney now belonged to Shafter's men.

The Americans who fought at El Caney were exhausted. They had either been marching or fighting for about twenty-five straight hours. General Lawton knew they were needed by Shafter at Santiago. Lawton gave his men time to cook coffee and to eat hardtack, then he had the necessary steel in his character to make them form on the road and march.

His advance guard was fired on. It was dark, and he feared an ambush. The road was unfamiliar, so Lawton marched the soldiers by a circuitous route. At eleven at night he let them sleep by the side of the road until three in the morning. Then they hiked on toward San Juan Heights.

When the rolls were checked it was discovered that General Vara had had only 520 soldiers. Of these, 235 were killed or wounded. General Lawton lost 81 men killed and 360 wounded out of the 6,553 soldiers General Shafter had made available.

Before Lawton left El Caney he had everyone help bury the dead. When he and his men left to join General Shafter in front of San Juan Hill, he gave a burial detail orders to bury General Vara's body with full military honors. On the Fourth of July at sunset the red rays of the tropical sun colored the wrecked stone fort and the battered blockhouses. As General Vara's body was placed in its grave, three volleys split the silence in a final salute to the fearless Spanish leader.

15 SAN JUAN HILL—AND A DILEMMA

I N THE meantime, the plan to capture Santiago was col-
lapsing. General Vara and his courageous fighters at El
Caney had upset the timetable. The situation was confused.

Along the muddy track that led through jungles and open
country to the city, eight thousand of Shafter's soldiers
waited for the go-ahead signal. The heat was stifling. There
seemed to be no air along the narrow road. The soldiers
crowded into the brush and dank grass to make way for
mounted messengers and staff officers, and for the Signal
Corps men pulling wire so that Shafter would have telephone
communication with his principal leaders during the battle.
The bugs seemed to regard the soldiers as fresh meat.

Fighting Joe Wheeler, suffering from fever, trotted up the
road to the dismounted cavalry brigade in order to see the
coming attack. When he arrived at the Rough Rider Regiment he felt so ill he had to lie down. Taking his place was
a veteran of thirty-seven years' service, Brigadier General
Sumner, who had been a captain in the Civil War.

The leaders of the long column of men on the jungle trail had problems. The Spanish were in trenches on the hills and, with just one narrow path leading to the front, all they had to do was to watch the trail's entrance and when the Americans appeared to aim and fire.

Brigadier General Adna Chaffee, hard-bitten cavalryman, planned to steer clear of the trap. His idea was to cut paths through the jungle and the tall brush of more open country so the troops could fan out and form for the attack quickly. This would avoid making a succession of targets appear on the jungle trail. However, General Shafter disapproved Chaffee's scheme because he felt he could not spare the time to cut the paths.

Shafter was becoming cranky. The heat and long hours under pressure made him ill. Nothing suited him and, like Wheeler, he would not give in. At about six thirty in the morning on July 1, Shafter called for his horse, struggled into the saddle, and rode a half-mile to the north so he could see the enemy's positions on the two hills. When he returned to his headquarters he almost fell from his horse. Nearby was Lieutenant Colonel McClernand, chief of staff, a veteran of the Indian wars.

"I'm sick," Shafter moaned. "You know the plan?"

"Yes, sir."

"Then carry it out. Send Miley forward to keep us informed. I'll join you later." Then Shafter all but fainted.

Shafter was not alone in suffering from the heat. Major Philip Reade, inspector general, reported, "Some men were insane with the heat . . . the animals were played out."

American field artillery from positions off the crowded trail opened up on the twin hills. The answer was dreadful.

It began to rain death on the Americans. Shrapnel shells bursting with a terrific crack at treetop height sprayed them with steel balls one-half inch in diameter. The rain of steel from the Spanish artillery plunged downward with such force that the shrapnel pellets could go through a man. Roosevelt was hit with one that merely raised a lump on his wrist. Presumably the shrapnel ball hit a tree branch first, otherwise he would have lost part of his hand. Men went down. The shrapnel shells bursting over the trees were a severe test for the soldiers because they had to stand and receive them, and because they could not fire back. The American artillery tried to answer the Spanish guns but the American guns could not compete; they were out of date, and again the black powder the Americans were using was a here-I-am signal.

In the confusion, the soldiers courageously moved out of the brush, formed on the trail, and marched toward the enemy. The Americans cast their horse-collar blanket rolls and haversacks to the side of the road, practically telling their equipment good-bye, because Cuban irregulars following the army picked them up.

The Signal Corps sent up a balloon with Lieutenant Colonel Derby as an observer. Great things were expected of this balloon, but it had little gas and was towed along just above the treetops, a huge marker for the enemy. Because Colonel Derby could see little and because the balloon was advertising the location of the troops, the order came to haul it down. A second later an enemy shell burst beside it and it came down crashing. The soldiers cheered. Fortunately, Derby was unhurt.

In the jungle's heavy brush, units were tangled. Privates found themselves with noncommissioned officers they had never seen before. Enemy sharpshooters, dressed in green, poured aimed fire from the treetops and from the sides of the trail. Cadet Ernest Haskell, who had been at West Point two years and, on furlough from the Academy, was now an acting second lieutenant in the Rough Riders, was shot through the stomach. Roosevelt sprang to the cadet's side and tried to help him. Roosevelt wrote later that Haskell said, "All right, Colonel. I am going to get well. Don't bother with me, and don't let any man [leave the firing line] with me." Roosevelt said that when he shook hands with the young man he thought he would surely die, yet he recovered.

Lieutenant Denis Michie, aide to the grandfatherly looking and fearless Brigadier General Hamilton Hawkins and former captain and coach of the first West Point football team, was shot dead. The Ninth Cavalry Regiment lost its colonel, John Hamilton. Buckey O'Neill, former sheriff and mayor of Prescott, Arizona, was telling a friend that "the bullet isn't made that can hit me," when that bullet whistled through the jungle, struck him in the mouth, and killed him. Colonel Egbert of the Sixteenth Infantry, at the head of his regiment, was severely wounded.

The excitement increased. Bullets seemed to be cracking everywhere. Wounded men were being carried to the rear on litters. The litter-bearers felt like targets in a shooting gallery.

Finally, units straggled into line along the San Juan River, where they could fire up at the Spaniards. The Spanish had a definite advantage. They were firing down on the Americans from their trenches, and they knew the range. Brigadier General Young wrote later of this trying time, "The coolest man I saw under fire was a Tenth Cavalryman, First Lieutenant John J. Pershing." (He would become a world-famous general in the First World War.)

A shell banged into the leading battalion of the 71st New York Volunteers just as it was leaving the trail for open country. Twelve men fell in a bloody, tangled heap. This was too much for the advance battalion. It turned and streaked for the rear. Confusion increased as the men from the 71st tore through other units. The panic-stricken men were stopped when Regular Army officers formed a cordon.

The situation was serious. Colonel Wikoff, commanding three regiments, fell dead. Brigadier General Hamilton Hawkins walked bravely about in the knee-length grass of a meadow near the San Juan River to calm the men. Ammunition was low. There seemed to be no plan. Few leaders knew exactly what was expected of their units. Obviously the enemy had to be driven from the twin hills. It seemed impossible.

Suddenly there was a rattling, hail-like sound, amplified a thousand times. It was the Gatlings. Second Lieutenant Parker had moved his rapid-fire guns recklessly forward. They were spraying the Spanish trenches. "The sound of the Gatlings, 'coffee grinders' we called 'em," one man wrote, "was the best sound I ever heard on a battlefield." Parker and his Gatlings not only saved hundreds of American lives, but the storm of bullets his guns put down on the Spanish trenches startled the Spaniards. They scrambled out of the trenches and ran toward the city.

The harassed Americans looked up. It was about four hundred yards from the San Juan River to the top of San Juan Hill, about three hundred yards to the top of the hill just east of it. The distances looked like miles.

General Hawkins gave an order to a bugler and when his musician sounded the "Charge," the general yelled, "Charge! Come on!" He ran up the slope of San Juan Hill toward its blockhouse. Younger soldiers quickly passed him. Numbers of subordinate commanders all along the line yelled, "Charge!" and led their soldiers upward on the run. The Gatling guns, which saved the day, ceased firing as the Americans charged up the slopes.

Colonel Roosevelt galloped up on horseback, his blue polka-dot handkerchief tied about his neck cowboy fashion. He made his horse leap a barbed wire fence in front of his regiment, then he headed up the slope. When he saw that he was not being followed he turned his horse, jumped the barbed wire again, and taunted his soldiers, "What are you? Cowards?"

One Rough Rider said, "You didn't give us any order." Others took out their bayonets and slashed the barbed wire. Roosevelt trotted again toward the hill and waved his hat. This time the Rough Riders and some Negroes of the Tenth Cavalry, fighting alongside the Rough Riders, surged after him.

That afternoon Theodore Roosevelt, like others who led their men forward, was a splendid American leader. However, the attack was like a game to him. He wrote home in a few days, "The charge was great fun."

About 550 Americans fell, either killed or wounded.

On the hill the Rough Riders found several huge kettles used in making sugar, and this gave the hill its name.

The Spaniards retreated into earthworks closer to the city, with no one pursuing them.

The United States Army, exhausted, hungry, and without food, stopped. It was a dark hour. The wounded were especially pitiful. They needed food. They were transported back to the field hospitals in dirty supply wagons because only a few ambulances were available. Food, when it did arrive, was not the type that would sustain great effort. It was hardtack, bacon, sugar, and coffee, and that was all. The doctors felt concerned about the wounded. Fortunately, Clara Barton and some of her Red Cross workers arrived. They had flour, salt, condensed milk, and meal, and made gallons of gruel for the sick and wounded.

What was the American Army going to do? When General Lawton put his tired men on the north side of the city, *both* sides had about thirteen thousand soldiers. The Americans needed more than that, with the defenders behind trenches and in blockhouses and forts.

At Army Headquarters Shafter, back in command after a

rest, was as irritable as an injured bear. However, he made sure that captive Spanish soldiers were treated kindly because he knew that humane treatment would eventually help his own soldiers, and in a demand that the city surrender—which was promptly refused—he let the Spanish know that he was caring for their prisoners as best he could.

When it became dark on the outpost line, the ugly crabs crawled out of their holes again. Firing started, not at the crabs but at imaginary Spaniards the sentries thought they saw attacking. Orders to cease firing, given to the guards, were not obeyed. It was dangerous and kept men awake. Tom Hall, in his *Fun and Fighting of the Rough Riders,* wrote that a loud voice, evidently an officer's, shouted from behind Kettle Hill, "Cease firing in the First Volunteer Cavalry!"

No one paid attention to the command. The owner of the voice shouted the same thing again. Roosevelt lost his temper. He could not stand a slur on the Rough Riders. He got up and shouted, "You ass, we are *not* firing!"

Intermittent Spanish artillery fire fell on the Americans for the next two days. Spanish sharpshooters returned to harass the Americans. One of the Gatlings, elevated as high as possible, fired about seven thousand bullets into the city at places where Parker thought the Spanish Army was. The American artillery answered the Spanish artillery, but feebly.

Inspector General Reade wrote, "Spanish deserters came over because of ill-treatment. . . . Their uniform: light blue blouse and trousers with fine white vertical stripes, straw hat and light weight shoes."

The leader of the Spanish in the besieged city was General José Toral; General Linares had been wounded. Boldly, Shafter demanded that Toral surrender to save further bloodshed and the distress "of many people." Shafter signed the letter "Your obedient servant."

Toral replied that the city would not be surrendered and,

equally courteous, signed his answer, "I am, yours, with great respect and consideration."

While the gloomy situation was at a stalemate, the problems of the Rough Riders were not enough to occupy Roosevelt. His idea of helping the Army was to write a personal letter to his friend Senator Lodge in Washington, asking him to send "every regiment and above all every battery possible." Roosevelt added that the senior American general was "poor" and too bulky to get to the front. In writing such a letter Roosevelt seemed panicky.

Shafter was exhausted and half sick. He wrote later, "I came near suffering a sun stroke. I was nauseated and very dizzy. During the battle I felt very ill but kept on my horse most of the day.... [Then] for four days I was unable to take food. I began to fear a serious illness." His frustration and his sickness made him irascible. He sent peevish demands to the navy. Shafter wanted it to force its way through the narrow, mined channel and to attack Cervera's fleet. Shafter wrote Sampson, "My losses very heavy... I am at a loss to see why the navy cannot work as well as the army...."

William Sampson did not rise to the quarrel. He explained politely that he would lose a number of warships and many sailors if he tried to steam through the fortified entrance of the harbor. Sweeping mines alone, under the enemy's guns, would be costly.

Shafter was so worried that he now cabled Secretary of War Alger and asked him to see Secretary of the Navy Long and have Mr. Long order Admiral Sampson into the harbor. Long told the admiral to help all he could but not to risk his warships.

Finally, Admiral Sampson said he would attempt forcing an entrance into the harbor, but warned Shafter that if he failed both the army and navy would be in worse circumstances.

The general now sent an officer into the Spanish defenses

under a flag of truce demanding again that Toral surrender, and asking him to instruct all foreign women and children to leave the city because he was going to bombard it. General Toral replied courteously that he would pass on the message but said, "This city will not surrender."

General Shafter felt the pressure of the vise he was in. With the yellow fever and hurricane season almost at hand, time was precious. The Spanish outnumbered him and more might arrive any day from other parts of the island. To do everything possible, he asked Sampson to steam closer to the harbor's entrance so his heavy guns could reach the city and help in the forthcoming bombardment.

There was anxiety at Shafter's headquarters. Where did the best course lie? He called a council of war of his generals, which he conducted stretched out on a farmhouse door that had been removed from its hinges. He wanted to find out if his leaders thought he should abandon his ring around the city. Perhaps, the sick general ventured, the army might retire to the vicinity of its supply base at Siboney. The four generals facing Shafter did not agree, so Shafter decided the army would remain in place and that he would consider the matter further. Shortly he cabled Secretary Alger that he would hold his present position. When word leaked out that General Shafter had been thinking of surrendering the hard-won ground, the morale of the soldiers sagged even more.

Now came a blow. On the third of July, 3,579 Spaniards marched along the Cobre Road into Santiago as reinforcements. General García and his rebels made no effort to stop them. This gave the defenders more soldiers than the attackers.

General Shafter and Admiral Sampson agreed to confer near Siboney, and while they were traveling toward one another, one of the most startling events of the entire war occurred.

16   THE NAVY'S FOURTH-OF-JULY PRESENT

THERE is a saying, "It rains on the enemy, too."

In Santiago the Spanish were experiencing an ordeal. The thirty thousand inhabitants were almost out of every kind of food except rice. The city, hemmed in by the United States Army and blockaded by the United States Navy, had little chance of outlasting the siege. Men and animals began to starve. The American Army had discovered the reservoir two miles north of the city and had cut off the water. Long lines of people formed at the artesian wells.

There was low morale in both the Spanish Army and the Spanish Navy. The soldiers had not been paid in several months, and the sailors knew that certain types of guns in the fleet did not have enough ammunition for a hard fight. There was also barely enough coal for a dash for freedom. About a thousand sailors and Marines were ashore, helping man the blockhouses and trenches. If they were withdrawn, the defense lines about the city would be weakened. In addition, there was friction between the kindly, jovial Admiral Cervera and the starchy General Blanco.

Blanco, in Havana, about four hundred miles away from the besieged city, was irritated because he considered himself more capable than Cervera. No one Spaniard was in command of the island.

The two leaders, true to Spanish tradition, were extraordinarily polite. They talked back and forth over the telegraph, using the customary velvet phrases of the day. For example, Cervera telegraphed Blanco:

I AM IN RECEIPT OF YOUR CABLE, AND THANK YOUR EXCELLENCY VERY MUCH FOR KIND WORDS IN MY BEHALF. I HAVE TO RESPECT YOUR EXCELLENCY'S OPINIONS WITHOUT DISCUSSING THEM. . . .

The reply was just as flowery.

Underneath the surface the two Spanish leaders were irritated with each other; each felt that he should be in command. Finally, General Blanco cabled the Spanish Government in Madrid, and the reply made him the Number One Spaniard on the island. This gave a general far removed from the scene authority over an admiral who was literally on the spot.

The two leaders were more direct when they talked to Madrid through the undersea cable. General Blanco reported that the United States blockading squadron was reduced to seven battleships and that Cervera's ships had an excellent occasion to get away. Cervera, who knew more about Sampson's squadron a few miles away than did the remote general, cabled Madrid:

IT IS ABSOLUTELY IMPOSSIBLE FOR [OUR] SQUADRON TO ESCAPE OVER THE CIRCUMSTANCES. . . . THIS IS ALSO THE OPINION OF THE COMMANDERS OF MY SHIPS. . . . IT IS NOT TRUE THAT THE BLOCKADING SQUADRON HAS BEEN REDUCED TO BUT SEVEN SHIPS. EVEN

SO, THE SIX BEST SHIPS REPRESENT A FORCE THREE TIMES MY
OWN. . . . THE AMERICANS ARE CLOSE TO THE HARBOR. . . . THEIR
SEARCHLIGHTS MAKE IT IMPOSSIBLE FOR ME TO ESCAPE.

Admiral Cervera went on to say that he would never order
his squadron to try to dash through the blockade, but that if
the sortie were ordered, he would obey. He concluded that
such a plan would result in useless sacrifice.

An oily telegram went from General Blanco asking Cervera
to consider him a comrade rather than a chief. Then came a
barb, a ridiculously unrealistic statement: IT SEEMS TO ME, AD-
MIRAL CERVERA, YOU EXAGGERATE THE DIFFICULTIES OF LEAVING
SANTIAGO. THERE IS NO NEED TO FIGHT. ALL YOU ARE ASKED TO DO
IS TO ESCAPE. . . . The telegram went on to suggest that Cervera leave at night. Cervera thought this impracticable because
each evening, as soon as the sun sank behind the hills, the
American fleet moved in closer and searchlights illuminated
the harbor's entrance. Blanco's weathervane mind was exposed. Just a month previously he had cabled the Minister of
War in Madrid about the inadequacy of Cervera's squadron.

Finally, Admiral Cervera was ordered to leave the harbor,
not only by General Blanco but by Madrid.

The admiral called his captains aboard his flagship and
arranged for the thousand sailors and Marines who were in the
blockhouses and trenches to return. It was to be a dash for freedom—or death—through the winding 1,110-yard channel into
water controlled by the American warships. When the crews
learned of the plan, they offered up prayers for their deliver-
ance. It was a solemn and tense time. Seldom have so many
men gambled their lives knowing they had such little chance
of surviving. The six Spanish warships carried 146 heavy guns;
the seven biggest American men-of-war had 225.

Cervera expected great loss, but he thought that his fastest
ship, the *Cristóbal Colon*, might escape. It did not seem right

to him to slip away on her when the other ships would probably be sent to the bottom, so he transferred his flag to the
slower *María Teresa*. This act was not lost on his sailors. When
it was discovered, cheer after cheer rang out for the brave and
unselfish leader.

To prepare the way, Cervera sent a small gunboat after dark
down the channel, giving its captain the dangerous job of removing mines that blocked the strait. The admiral plotted a
western course, hoping to reach Cienfuegos, a port of thirty
thousand, or the capital, Havana, a seaport eight times as large.

This was a nervous time for the sailors. They believed, however, that their ships could outrun the American warships, with
the exception of the armored cruiser *Brooklyn*, which could
cut the water at nineteen and a half knots. The plan called for
each Spanish captain, after his ship eased by the wrecked *Merrimac*, to demand every pound of steam his engine room could
produce. The American warships, lying in dead water, would
have steam ready, but they were bound to lose valuable minutes
going from speed zero to full speed.

On the *María Teresa*, two hours after breakfast on July 3,
1898, a bugle blew. The armored cruiser raised its anchor and
led the way to the torturous channel. After the cruisers, which
were about eight hundred yards apart, came the ships the
Americans dreaded: the two torpedo-boat destroyers. Under
Cervera's leadership, the Spanish fleet was determined to fight
its way to the open sea.

It was hazy in the early morning, but the tropical sun burned
off the mist and gave the sea a glassy appearance. It was a
superb day.

This Sunday appeared to be another dull watch for the
crews of the blockading ships. The battleship *Massachusetts*
and the armed ship *Suwanee* pulled away to Guantánamo for
coal.

Up from the signal bridge of the *New York* went flags that meant: *"Disregard motions of commander-in-chief."*

The flagship *New York* steamed east toward Siboney, carrying Admiral Sampson toward his meeting with General Shafter. The Admiral knew that, if the Spaniards chose this day to fight their way out, his plan of attack would be followed. His orders were, "If the enemy tries to escape, close range at once and endeavor to sink his vessels or run them ashore."

The admiral was dressed for his horseback ride to meet the general: blue trousers thrust into khaki leggings and steel spurs clasping his heels. He not looking forward to his ride. He was tired of the long strain he had been under since he first sailed to Cuban waters from Key West.

When the admiral left the iron semicircle, Commodore Schley, on the armored cruiser *Brooklyn,* automatically became commander of the blockade. Schley, world famous for his rescue of Greely and his six companions from the Arctic, had graduated from the Naval Academy one year ahead of Admiral Sampson, but Sampson had been promoted faster than Schley.

At 9:35 A.M. the battleship *New York* was about six miles east of the blockade.

Because it was the first Sunday in the month, the captains on the blockading ships were preparing to read the Articles of War to their crews, refreshing them in the laws and rules of conduct in the Navy. The ships' chaplains were ready to follow with church services.

Suddenly a lookout on the *Brooklyn* yelled at the top of his voice, "Tell the commodore that the Spanish fleet is coming out!"

Schley tore for the conning tower. "General Quarters" sounded. Alarm bells clanged. Sailors and Marines jumped down iron stairways to their battle stations, and in their haste some were injured.

The Americans were momentarily surprised and handicapped. They had not expected Cervera to risk his ships in daylight. The Spaniards had the advantage. It would take the blockading ships about ten minutes to overcome inertia and to get under way.

Near Siboney, the *New York* had just lowered its best launch in the water so Admiral Sampson could go ashore. When a lookout saw the Spanish fleet emerging back near Morro Castle, the battleship did not wait to pick up its launch, but made a 180-degree-turn and headed at full steam for the Spaniards.

On the *Texas*, Naval Chaplain Jones wrote later, "I looked out of a port and saw the biggest ships I had ever seen in my life.... Cervera's magnificent ships of war. The first twelve-inch shell the men sent up was for Lieutenant Haesler's gun. The men down in the magazine had chalked on her, '*In memory* of the MAINE from her beloved sister ship TEXAS....' "

The battleship *Iowa*, looking right into the throat of the harbor, opened fire with a six-inch gun at the *María Teresa*. At the same moment the guns of the *Oregon* roared at the Spanish war vessel. Because it was a lone target, the *María Teresa* suffered. Nevertheless, she tore directly for the *Brooklyn* to ram her.

The *Brooklyn*'s navigating officer sang out to Commodore Schley, "They are coming right at us!" The commodore yelled back, "Go right for them!" The forward turret of the *Brooklyn* thundered. The three unusually tall funnels of the American warship sent up tremendous clouds of black smoke. The cruiser moved forward slowly toward its adversary. Signal flags clattered to the deck. Spanish fire had cut the halyards.

The U.S. warship nearest to the *María Teresa* was the *Texas*, now about fifteen hundred yards away. She punished the *María*. A shell crashed into the *María's* steering gear and she altered her course, steaming west. Other Spanish ships were now out of the harbor's mouth. They also headed west. It was a running fight.

An officer on the dreaded Spanish destroyer *Plutón* wrote afterwards, ". . . Our first ships out used smoke producing powder to try to hide the others but it rose in fleecy clouds to make our position all the plainer to the enemy. A shell from the *Brooklyn*, I think, literally stove us in pieces. It passed through the boiler room letting out steam and scalding water upon the crew, to stab them like sword-blades. . . . Where the *Oregon* came from, out of the sea that morning, I can't imagine; and how she traveled so fast is an enigma. I could not believe that any battleship afloat could chase and corner our *Cristóbal Colon*, a twenty-one knot cruiser. . . .

"A shell from the forward turret of the *Brooklyn* struck us in the bow, plowing down amidships. Then it exploded. It tore down the bulkheads, destroyed stanchions, crippled two rapid fire guns, killed fifteen or twenty men, and carried panic everywhere. Cervera ordered one of our gun crews to concentrate on the *Brooklyn's* steering gear. . . . In vain! One of the *Iowa's* shells struck the eleven-inch gun in the forward turret of the [*Plutón*], cutting a furrow as clean as a knife out of the side of the gun. The shell exploded halfway in the turret, making the whole vessel stagger and shake in every plate. . . . Even the machinery was clogged by corpses. The place was slippery from blood. . . . There were so many wounded the surgeons ceased trying to dress the wounds.

"Shells exploded inside the ship setting fire to the wood-work, and even the hospital was turned into a furnace. The first wounded . . . sent there had to be abandoned by the surgeons, who fled for their lives from the intolerable heat. . . . The whole gun deck of [our cruiser] *Vizcaya* was in flames.

We knew her magazines would go up any minute. She was headed for the shore, where the *María Teresa* had already gone. . . . A shot from the *Texas* exploded a torpedo on the *Vizcaya* and killed eighty men and made her a complete wreck. In the meantime the survivors from the flagship were jumping into the sea to escape. . . . Admiral Cervera himself threw off all of his clothes but two garments and finally leaped into the sea, where he was supported by his son. . . ."

The *Colon* signaled that further fighting was useless and crashed into the shore.

The Spanish fleet was wrecked. The battle had lasted but three hours and forty-five minutes. When the *Texas* steamed near the beach where the *Vizcaya* was burning, Captain Philip called from the bridge of the *Texas*, "Don't cheer, boys. The poor devils are dying!" Americans who had worked so hard to destroy the enemy fleet now labored to rescue the fearless Spanish sailors. When the *New York* steamed into the mess of struggling Spaniards, a coxswain on the battleship, anxious to throw a life preserver overboard, could find none, so he heaved over the side the chaplain's wooden pulpit.

Fighting Bob Evans, skipper of the *Iowa*, said what many American sailors thought, "Surely, no braver sight was ever seen than when these gallant little paper shells actually returned the fire of the battleships."

Boats from the *Iowa*, the torpedo boat *Ericsson*, and other American war vessels, rescued many Spanish sailors, the *Harvard* working until 9:45 P.M. When Captain Antonio Eulate, wounded and exhausted, was lifted to the deck of the *Iowa* in a bosun's chair, Captain Evans received him with honors due his rank. Eulate kissed his sword good-bye and presented it to Fighting Bob, who returned it. Later Eulate cabled his wife in Puerto Rico, "SHIP BURNED, LIFE AND HONOR SAVED."

Randolph Hearst, on his yacht, flagship for news reporters, also helped rescue Spanish sailors.

When the *New York* pulled up near the rest of the fleet, Commodore Schley felt hurt because Admiral Sampson had not sent a message of congratulation. Nearly everyone expected the admiral would signal, *"Well done,"* but no flags appeared on the halyards of the flagship. Sampson was the more efficient naval officer of the two, but he was bitterly disappointed not to have been actively in command when the Spanish ships tried to escape.

Schley sent up the signal, *"This is a great day for our country."* There was a brief acknowledgment by Sampson. That was all. Then Commodore Schley had a launch lowered and chugged to the *New York* to make the amazing report to the admiral that during the fighting only one American was killed.* When Schley's launch traveled to the flagship, the crews of every American warship cheered him, save the crew of the *New York*. It reflected the admiral's attitude.

That afternoon, Admiral Sampson sent a message to Washington:

THE FLEET UNDER MY COMMAND OFFERS THE NATION AS A FOURTH OF JULY PRESENT THE WHOLE OF CERVERA'S FLEET. IT ATTEMPTED TO ESCAPE AT 9:30 THIS MORNING. AT TWO THE LAST SHIP, THE CRISTÓBAL COLON, HAD RUN ASHORE SEVENTY-FIVE MILES WEST OF SANTIAGO AND HAULED DOWN HER COLORS. THE INFANTA MARÍA TERESA, OQUENDO, AND THE VIZCAYA WERE FORCED ASHORE, BURNED AND BLOWN UP WITHIN 20 MILES OF SANTIAGO. THE FUROR AND PLUTÓN WERE DESTROYED WITHIN 4 MILES OF THAT PORT.

W. T. SAMPSON

This inspiring bulletin touched off Fourth-of-July celebrations across the nation, although some thought it overly dramatic. But to General Shafter and his worn-out soldiers, fac-

* Chief Yeoman George H. Ellis, of the *Brooklyn*.

ing the barbed wire about Santiago, the destruction of Cervera's fleet was of the greatest importance.

The American Army was exhilarated by the momentous victory of the United States Navy. Shafter sent a messenger under the protection of a white flag into the city to inform Toral that the Spanish fleet was destroyed, and that Cervera was aboard the armed U.S. yacht *Gloucester* as a captive. Anxious to defeat his enemy with the loss of as few Americans as possible, Shafter "suggested" that Toral reconsider and surrender, but Toral refused. "This place will not be surrendered," he said.

Then an act of war stampeded thousands of citizens of Santiago. At midnight on July 4–5, the iron cruiser *Reina Mercedes*, the last Spanish ship in the harbor, tried to escape. Projectiles from three battleships, the *Texas, Massachusetts,* and *Indiana,* roared into her. The hapless cruiser sank. The noise of the guns reverberated into Santiago. Fifteen thousand terrified people, half of the city's population, swarmed out of town in panic to escape what they thought was a bombardment.

It was a shocking scene. The sick, the very elderly, and women with tiny babies were carried in chairs and in beds. The frightened people hiked four miles to El Caney. "That place," Robert Mason, British Vice Consul, wrote, "was stinking with half-buried corpses of men and horses." In three days the people began to starve. The American Red Cross tried to help, but it was swamped. Mason said food was so precious that five biscuits sold for five dollars. Shafter sent food to the poor refugees, but the ability of the army was taxed.

General Shafter felt anxious. The Spanish were penned up in the city, and it seemed utterly implausible that the American army could not cash in on the navy's victory. Although army reinforcements arrived, the General lacked artillery that could help his infantrymen drive past the blockhouses and over the trenches into the city. A straight-ahead attack that would cost the lives of thousands was not for him.

He was in serious trouble. Malaria, typhoid, and dysentery were shrinking his army. The doctors warned that the yellow-fever season was present and said if the army stayed in this part of Cuba it would suffer unforeseeable casualties, the dreaded disease knocking men down as if it were a bomb. In a Michigan regiment at Siboney there were already three cases of the horrible fever. Orders went out to those who knew of this outbreak of yellow fever to keep it quiet. Downpours of rain, and billions of mosquitoes arriving in clouds shortly after each sunset, made Shafter's soldiers miserable.

With rains turning the roads into rivers of mud and the fifteen thousand refugees overburdening the supply system, starvation of the United States Army was not an impossibility. Then, too, it was hurricane time; a devastating storm would drive away incoming supply ships. It seemed to the harassed general that the answer to his problems lay in the navy's forcing past the forts guarding the entrance to the harbor and attacking the city at close range.

Admiral Sampson was not about to lose his warships, and refused the idea. The argument carried all the way to the White House, where it was placed before President McKinley. He sidestepped the dispute, sending back word for the general and the admiral to confer. It appeared that Mr. McKinley was avoiding the issue, but his order to Sampson and Shafter developed the answers to General Shafter's harrowing problems.

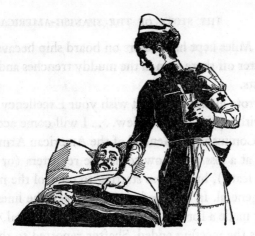

17   VICTORY—AND FEVER

THE two leaders conferred. William Sampson said, "As a last resort the fleet will force its way into the harbor, but first I think we should bombard the city."

For two days in mid-July the United States Army and Navy combined to send hundreds of shells cracking into Santiago. Although the bombardment sounded as if the end of the world had come, it did little damage because many of the buildings were of stone. Naval bombardment is a terrifying thing. The thunderlike clap of the shells petrified the fifteen thousand people in the city.

When Shafter sent another surrender demand to Toral, the Spaniard said he would consider it if the United States would transport the Spanish Army to Spain. The correspondence became so flowery that Toral was addressing Shafter as "Excellency" and "Your Eminence." General Toral agreed to consult General Blanco.

During an armistice General Nelson Miles, senior General of the United States Army, who had been released from "confinement" in Washington by Mr. Alger, arrived with reinforcements. Miles kept his soldiers on board ship because they were far better off there than in the muddy trenches and fever-ridden forests.

Shafter wrote his adversary, "I wish your Excellency would honor me with a personal interview. . . . I will come accompanied by the Commanding General of the American Army. . . ." Shafter was at a loss as to how to handle reporters (or he did not want to learn), but he was starting to control the mind of the enemy general. In the conference between the lines, William Shafter made a forceful impression on José Toral.

As soon as the meeting ended, Shafter reported to the War Department, ending his telegram ominously: THERE IS A GOOD DEAL OF NERVOUSNESS THROUGHOUT THE ARMY ON ACCOUNT OF YELLOW FEVER WHICH IS CERTAINLY AMONG US.

At this time no one knew exactly how malaria or yellow fever started or spread. In 1898 the United States Marine Hospital Service reported that yellow fever was spread "by the infection of places and articles of bedding, clothing, and furniture—or in some obscure manner."

There was no doubt what yellow fever did to its victim. The unfortunate person vomited blood and suffered yellow jaundice, severe prostration and muscular pain. The liver and digestive tracts were attacked. Although it is a disease of the tropics, epidemics had occurred in Philadelphia, New York, and Boston. One of the worst outbreaks took place in New Orleans eleven years before the Civil War, when 29,020 cases broke out, with 8,101 deaths, a mortality rate of 27.91 percent.

In 1898 Dr. Giovanni Battista Grassi, a zoologist, took time from his studies of the animal kingdom to try to free Italy from its greatest scourge: malaria. In September he announced it was a certain type of mosquito that carried the disease, the *Anopheles*, which attacked the red blood corpuscles and gave its victims excruciating fever and chattering teeth. However, this was unknown in Cuba in July. It was obvious to Shafter and his officers that the greatest enemy the army faced was fever.

When General Miles heard of the large numbers of Americans ill from malaria, he ordered some of the homes and buildings in Siboney burned, thinking it would stop the spread of the disease. This upset the Cubans in that area. They said it was worse to have the Americans around than Butcher Weyler.

At the "capitulation" talks that followed between the lines, General Toral was represented by two Spanish officers and by the British Vice Consul. Shafter's commissioners were Fighting Joe Wheeler, Henry Lawton, and John Miley.

For three days the commissioners met and discussed the situation. American officers feared the conferences would amount to nothing and might be a Spanish trick. Subordinates urged General Shafter to wait no longer but to attack. He refused to be stampeded, believing that he could persuade General Toral to surrender without more fighting. Colonel Roosevelt took no chances. He ordered his Rough Riders to build bombproof dugouts and to dig a zigzag trench to a key blockhouse. He said the idea that there might be a "brush with the Spaniards" kept the men interested.

Late at night on July 15, 1898, Toral wrote Shafter that he could *capitulate* if the United States would agree to transport Spanish soldiers in the district to Spain as soon as possible. When the letter came, Lieutenant Miley wrote, "Words cannot express the feeling of relief."

The negotiations between Shafter and Toral brought the siege of Santiago to an end, because Toral decided to surrender. Twelve thousand Spanish soldiers in Santiago, near Guantánamo, and in other places in the eastern province laid down their arms. Shafter and his senior generals were thankful, their soldiers delighted.

Spanish garrisons dotted the map of the island, but the

Spaniards indicated they wanted no more war. In giving in, the Spanish had no idea of the forlorn condition of the American army.

Shafter's ill health still had him under pressure. One foot was swollen from gout, and he rode about with it in a gunny sack. He quarreled with Sampson over who would take charge of a Spanish gunboat captured in the harbor, and refused to allow Captain Chadwick, U.S.N., Sampson's representative, to sign the Articles of Capitulation. Shafter wrote testily, "When the navy captured the Spanish fleet no claim for any credit was made by the army."

He was also upset with García because the Cuban was not always aggressive. García boycotted the surrender formation, moving into the interior with his little army.

The ceremony of surrender contained more action than anyone envisioned because of Shafter's irritableness.

To witness the surrender, all the regiments were drawn up in line along the tops of their trenches. Shafter and his senior leaders, escorted by one hundred horsemen, rode out to a huge ceiba tree between the lines. The magnificent "silk cotton" tree had sheltered the commissioners during their meetings. Out came General Toral and his staff, accompanied by one hundred smartly dressed infantrymen. The two sides exchanged salutes, and Toral formally surrendered the eastern division of Cuba and Santiago. Shafter presented Toral with the sword and spurs of the dead hero, General Vara de Rey. Then the two leaders and their entourage traveled to the Governor's palace in the city. Two hours before Toral had saluted the red-and-yellow banner of Spain and hauled it down.

At twelve o'clock Captain Capron's battery fired twenty-one guns while bands played the national airs of Spain and of the United States.* Two companies of United States infantry

---

* Captain Capron—father of Allyn Capron, Jr., killed at Las Guasimas.

presented arms. Shafter's aides, Captain McKittrick and Lieutenant Miley, and Fighting Joe Wheeler's aide, his son, Lieutenant Joseph Wheeler, Jr., raised the American flag on the roof of the palace.

Suddenly, Shafter's dislike of newspaper writers boiled over. Mr. Sylvester Scovil, an aggressive reporter, was up on the roof where he could photograph the scene. Shafter thought Scovil spoiled the tableau. The general shouted, "Miley! Tell that man to get off there."

Lieutenant Miley indicated that Scovil had refused to leave. Shafter, who was now on foot, turned to two soldiers and said, "Go up there and throw him off!"

The soldiers left to obey, but Mr. Scovil rushed down and in deep anger charged the general and tried to hit him. Fortunately Scovil missed. Infantrymen grabbed Scovil and moved him through the crowd to a niche in a wall where a statue had stood. They hoisted him to the statue's place, kept him there until the ceremony was over, then escorted him to the guardhouse, where he was kept for a short time.

The Spanish Army turned in its arms and marched to San Juan and Kettle Hills, where they made a camp.

Both the United States Army and Navy, with some help by the Spaniards, worked to make sure there were no mines in the channel to the harbor so that supply ships could enter. The Americans were astounded by the desolation, poverty, and filth in the town. It was one of the dirtiest cities on the face of the globe.

To get the news of the surrender to outlying garrisons in the province, General Shafter sent his dependable special helper, Lieutenant Miley, on a twelve-day expedition into wild, almost trackless country. With Miley rode an officer from Toral's staff (who bore a letter signed by Toral), two troops of cavalry for protection, and a pack train bearing supplies. They found poverty among the Cubans, people who lived in fear of their enemies.

On July 25, 1898, General Miles and five thousand soldiers landed on the south coast of Puerto Rico. They planned to expel completely the Spaniards from the West Indies. General Miles handled the newspapermen far more considerately than Shafter, yet Miles saw that news reports from the United States reached the enemy. Consequently he informed Washington that he would land at Point Fajardo, on the east coast, and the papers printed it. By doing this but landing on the south coast, he fooled the Spanish general, who rushed some troops to Point Fajardo. In twenty days Miles ran up the flag over the Puerto Rican capital.

Back in camp near Santiago, fevers were torturing William Shafter's soldiers. Lieutenant Rhodes wrote in his diary:

July 27, 1898. . . . The sick are increasing at a fearful rate. Some 250 are on sick report in two regiments, an increase of 34 over yesterday, with 60 new cases of fever.
July 28, 1898. . . . McGoldrick died at 4:40 this morning. Saw Chaplain Springer and arranged for the funeral at 8:00 A.M. Decided on no "funeral honors" on account of the depressing effect upon many of the men. . . .

The soldiers in their heavy blue uniforms, far more suitable to the Canadian Rockies, felt miserable. Some of their troubles came from that and from lying in muddy trenches under a tropical sun and in drenching rains with no shelter. Numbers of the seriously ill were shipped to Siboney by railroad freight car which the soldiers nicknamed "The Yellow Fever Express." When extra uniforms became available from supply ships, the clothing the sick had been wearing was tossed on bonfires in an effort to stop the spread of the fevers.

About four thousand soldiers were sick by the end of July.

With more and more of his soldiers becoming ill, Shafter tried to persuade the War Department to order his army home, but the authorities in Washington could not visualize the scene.

Shafter called a conference. All of his generals attended except Hamilton Hawkins, who had been wounded in the foot, and the gigantic Sam Young, who was ill. General Shafter made sure the tempestuous Colonel Roosevelt was present. In the meeting sat three winners of the Medal of Honor: Adelbert Ames, Leonard Wood, and Henry W. Lawton.

The outcome was an amazing document, a "Round Robin" letter, signed by the eleven officers, that warned of the yellow-fever peril in strong terms. It went on to say, ". . . This army must be moved at once or it will perish. . . . Persons responsible for preventing such a move will be responsible for the unnecessary loss of many thousands of lives. . . ." The Round Robin declared that the observations were based on the unanimous opinion of the medical officers with the army in Cuba.

General Lawton wrote below the signatures that he considered the language too strong, and that he thought "much of the fatal illness was due to homesickness and other depressing influences."

The document violated precedent: long custom forbade military men from banding together to sign a joint letter, but the Round Robin brought results. The eleven signers addressed it to General Shafter, who forwarded it to the War Department. It was obvious that the letter would be a bombshell when it arrived in the United States.

Shortly after the signing, Teddy Roosevelt informed William Shafter that an Associated Press reporter wanted a copy. Shafter said, "I don't care whether the gentleman has it or not." It was the first case on record of Shafter's calling a newswriter a gentleman.

President McKinley first learned of the explosive letter when he read his evening paper. He immediately called Secretary

Alger. Both were angry. They and the officers in the War Department were hurt because they thought the letter reflected on their work. When more newspapers printed it, many Americans became upset, particularly parents of the soldiers and their wives and sweethearts.

Mr. Alger quickly ordered the army to move at once to Montauk Point, New York, at the tip of Long Island, because it was thought that a cool climate would help the sufferers. Vessels began to arrive in Santiago to transport the disrupted army. To take its place in Cuba, "immune regiments," volunteers from Southern states, thought to be immune to yellow fever, arrived.

New scandals developed. Major Philip Reade, an inspector general, wrote down carefully what he saw and sent it to the War Department. When Alger saw Reade's report he was livid and ordered every copy destroyed. However, one copy was secreted and ended up at West Point. Part of Reade's report read:

...A good medical authority in Cuba says that if [Shafter's Army] is kept here from 20 to 70% will be dead by October 1....

The 1st Division hospital, Doctor M. W. Wood's, consists of 3 hospital tents, 5 extra flies, 7 cots, 8 blankets, no mattresses or pillows. Major Wood said, "The suffering and misery of this Division cannot be overstated. We hear their moans at night as they lie side by side at the well. They have no change of clothing, no blankets, insufficient food. The supply of medical stores is insufficient. The surgeons are overworked. There is plenty of food aboard the transports less than five miles away.... Humanity demands that these sick be transferred to a vessel fitted up as a hospital ship....

The honest inspector went on to report, "The soldiers vomited at the sight of a label of [canned] beef. It is either spoiled or has no nourishment.... Malaria patients are stretched on the ground.... No regiment has more than one medical officer for duty.... Heavy rains, gumbo mud...."

When the ships arrived to transport the army to Montauk Point, many of the vessels were filthy. The wounded suffered the most. On the *Seneca*, called a horror ship by some writers, war correspondent Harrie Hancock wrote, "The water was two months old. In a glass of it a thick red precipitate settled. Wounded men often asked for a glass of 'white water.'"

Major Reade, in his suppressed report, wrote of the nine days' voyage:

On the *Seneca* there are no hospital attendants aboard to look after the wounded. One doctor, Dr. Hicks, works all hours of the day and night. Newspaper correspondents and attachés are occupying staterooms with the wounded lying on deck.... The wounds are never dressed. The doctor said we have no instruments or medicines.... The ships *Relief* and *Concho* are just as bad....

Alger did not have the moral courage to let the report circulate. Actually it reflected on the American people, who had rushed to war without being prepared.

Although he banned the report, some of the correspondents wrote of the horrible conditions, and when the first wounded who were able to write letters home described the trip to Montauk Point, authorities in Washington worried. A tart telegram came to Shafter from the War Department asking why this was allowed to happen. General Shafter blew up. He wired back, WE DID THE BEST WE COULD UNDER THE CIRCUMSTANCES.... He ended his message with a blast, I WILL NOT QUIETLY SUBMIT TO HAVING THE ONUS LAID ON ME OF THE LACK OF THESE HOSPITAL FACILITIES.

When the first group of twenty-nine transports arrived at Montauk Point, more difficulties appeared. There was no camp to receive the weary men. Also, they were landed a few miles from the place where the camp was being built, and numbers could barely drag themselves over the distance. It was hard to rush supplies to Montauk Point because the railroad had only a single track. It was discovered, too, that wells had to be dug, and until they were ready, tank cars would have to haul water from Jamaica, on the western part of Long Island. At great expense more carpenters, electricians, plumbers, and other skilled workers were rushed to Montauk to finish the camp. Then some of the workers went on strike.

During the first week there was chaos, but a creditable camp soon took shape on the rolling dunes covered with scrub oaks and pines. It was named Camp Wikoff in honor of the infantry colonel who was killed at San Juan Hill.

The doctors reported that most of the army's cooks could not prepare food adequately for sick men, so wealthy people sent their chefs, as well as hundreds of dollars' worth of delicacies. The Red Cross also rushed to the aid of the sick by providing nurses, cots, clothing, and special food.

In 1898, Montauk was the greatest name in the American cattle industry. Roosevelt was entranced with the picturesque ranch and made the ranch house his headquarters.* He knew what to say and how to dramatize himself. When newspaper reporters sought him out and asked how he felt, he said, "I feel disgracefully well."

To the camp came President McKinley. He moved about escorted by Colonel Roosevelt and a troop of cavalry. The President endeared himself to the soldiers by visiting the hospitals and by going from cot to cot to shake hands with the men and to thank them.

When the Volunteers were well enough to leave Montauk and its beautiful beaches, they were sent home. Colonel Roosevelt's army career had ended. On September 15 he

* In 1898 the ranch had no official name. Today it is called Deep Hollow Ranch.

delivered a sermon exhorting his Rough Riders to behave in civilian life and telling them how proud he was to have been their colonel. The regiment presented him with a Frederic Remington bronze, "The Broncobuster." He shook hands with each Rough Rider, wishing him Godspeed. It was a moving, sentimental moment, particularly for the leader, Roosevelt.

When soldiers in Regular Army units were well enough to move, they were transferred to Army posts.

The camp at Montauk served a splendid purpose, aiding men in recovering from tropical fevers and wounds, as well as exertions in Cuba and Puerto Rico. Before the camp was disbanded, between 20,000 and 35,000 soldiers had rested there, most of them regaining their health.

On the other side of the world, in Manila, the war wound up with but little fighting. The Spaniards in the Philippines seemed almost as glad as those in Cuba to be returning to Spain. However, more fighting broke out when the Filipino leader, Aguinaldo, who acted as if he were an emperor, began to fight American soldiers. He and his followers believed that the United States had promised freedom for the Philippines.

A treaty of peace between the United States and Spain was signed in Paris on December 10, 1898, and Spain received $20,000,000. It was not clear what this was for. Presumably it reimbursed Spain for investments in the Philippines.

Senator Cushman K. Davis, chairman of the Foreign Relations Committee, in discussing the United States' new role in the Pacific, said, "We will not pull the flag down in Hawaii."

The war strengthened friendship between Great Britain and the United States. Englishmen followed the war as if they were involved, and cheered each U.S. victory.

The United States, emerging as a power in world affairs, faced new problems and difficulties. Ownership of the 7,083 islands of the Philippines, an area about the size of Ohio, with a mixture of native races, meant involvement in the Far East. The treaty of peace was the formal ending of a four months' war that demanded great sacrifices from the soldiers.

Although only about twenty thousand Americans actually fired at the enemy, many times that number received pensions. It was an expensive war, costing about $250,000,000 even before the first pension was awarded. Three hundred and sixty-one United States soldiers died in battle, and 2,565 perished from other causes. Many others suffered from wounds. More than 90 percent of the casualties were caused by disease. The Spanish were not anxious to reveal their casualties.

The war relegated Spain to the status of a second-class power. Psychologically it unified the United States after it had been ripped apart by the Civil War.

Fortune had blessed Shafter's army. If the Spanish general in the Santiago area had possessed an aggressive nature, and if he had had better intelligence as to the state of Shafter's army, the United States soldiers could have been pushed into the sea.

18 AFTERMATH

WHEN General Shafter addressed the Chamber of Commerce in Los Angeles after the war, some of his former soldiers were in the audience. The crowd rose to its feet and yelled as the portly general climbed slowly up the stairs to the stage. When they were quiet, he said, in his homely way, that he had done only what he had been paid to do. He said he was thunderstruck when, between the lines at Santiago, General Toral said he would surrender twelve thousand Spanish soldiers who were beyond his reach. Shafter went on to say that, with the capture of 15 percent of her army in Cuba and the destruction of the fleet, Spain surrendered because she realized she had no chance to win.

The general recalled the voyage to Cuba. "I had with me a number of foreign attachés. They predicted disaster." The crowd almost drowned out his words with applause. He spoke of the splendid work of the doctors and of the handicaps under which they had worked. He gave credit to Dr. Good-fellow, of his staff, for suggesting during the surrender talks that wounded Spanish prisoners be returned to the Spanish lines. Twenty-seven ambulance loads were sent back. Shafter said, "They were received with the greatest joy. The story these men told of the kind treatment they had received made the Spanish see that if they surrendered they would be treated in a civilized manner."

In conclusion, Shafter said, "I hate to see one foot of territory which has been paid for by American blood and treasure given up." It was something many Americans thought.

No student of the war can fail to be impressed with Shafter's eagerness to win, coupled with his concern that he lose as few soldiers as possible.

The conduct of the war received little applause elsewhere. Investigation followed investigation. Searches looked into everything from "embalmed beef" to the War Department. It became obvious that unpreparedness for war, coupled with a desire to fight, had caused many of the difficulties.

A long-drawn-out investigation, featured in magazines and newspapers and known as the Sampson-Schley Controversy intrigued the public. Almost everyone took sides. Although Winfield Schley's indecisive work off Cuba before the Spanish warships were blockaded was finally exposed, most people thought this warm and friendly man a hero of the war. William Sampson, colder but perhaps the more efficient of the two, had alienated people by not mentioning the commodore's name in his reports of the battle off Santiago. However, the top naval authority of the time, Admiral Mahan, said that credit for the victory belonged to Admiral Sampson because the battle was fought according to his plan.

In the summer of 1901, with more and more being written about the naval battle, Schley, now a retired admiral, felt his name had been slurred and demanded a court of inquiry.

This was a mistake because the court, after a three-month investigation, announced that Schley had exhibited "vacillation, dilatoriness, and lack of enterprise." Admiral Dewey, president of the court, upheld him. Schley felt bad over the court's verdict, but he took comfort in Dewey's opinion.

Theodore Roosevelt, who became President of the United States when McKinley was assassinated, now became involved in the offshoots of the controversy when General Miles criticized the court of inquiry by siding with Dewey. The idea of the senior general of the Army criticizing the naval court infuriated Roosevelt. The Secretary of War, now Elihu Root, gave Miles a reprimand "by direction of the President of the United States."

Old soldier Miles was dreadfully hurt. To attempt to remove this blot from his record he went to see President Roosevelt. Roosevelt spoke sharply to him for what he considered a "breach of discipline."

Theodore Roosevelt had traveled a glamorous trail since the declaration of war. More had been written about his exploits in Cuba than about any other army officer's. Everyone wanted to read about "Roosevelt of the Rough Riders." Correspondents in Cuba had doted on him because he had time for them and because he was a colorful, impulsive, and natural leader. A member of his family is said to have characterized him: "Father was unhappy unless he was the bride at the wedding or the corpse at the funeral."

He delighted in dramatizing himself. When he toured New York State in his successful campaign for the governorship, he had seven Rough Riders aboard his special train. He wore a Rough Rider's hat and waved it at the crowds who came to hear him speak. Before he appeared on the rear platform of the observation car at whistle-stops, a bugler blew the "Charge." Colonel Roosevelt began his talks to the voters in purple prose: "I heard that trumpet tear the tropic dawn when it summoned us to fight at Santiago."

He was disappointed at failing to win the Medal of Honor. He had been recommended for it by General Sumner for "gallantry and fearlessness" at San Juan and Kettle Hills, and General Leonard Wood also recommended him for it because of his "inspiring leadership." Roosevelt collected letters from important military leaders in support of stories of his bravery. He even had his friend Senator Lodge write President McKinley to urge that the Medal be presented, but Roosevelt did not receive it.

He carried his energy and impulsiveness into the White House. His fearlessness helped him initiate a hunt for "malefactors of great wealth." In seven and one half years in office, Roosevelt brought twenty-five formal charges against trusts before the courts. He became the champion of the average man. He protected the Western Hemisphere against encroachment by the Germans, who had their eyes on Venezuela, warning Kaiser Wilhelm and ordering the fleet under Admiral Dewey to be prepared for action. The Germans withdrew.

The two months it had taken the battleship *Oregon* to steam around the Horn made it evident that the United States needed a canal through the Isthmus of Panama. Roosevelt took drastic and forceful action to enable the canal to be dug.

The subjugation of the Philippines was also a major problem for the President. After the withdrawal of the Spaniards from the islands, Filipino-American relations rapidly deteriorated. Cruel guerrilla warfare broke out, with both sides becoming guilty of atrocities. It was jungle fighting with ambush easy. General Otis, the American commander in the islands, employed 47,000 soldiers over a period of eleven months to scatter Aguinaldo's army. It required more than two years of additional fighting to pacify the islands.

One of the oddities of the Philippine Insurrection was the difference in weapons. The Filipinos often fought in a lightning attack with bolo and kris, the latter a wavy-edged sword capable of inflicting horrible wounds. In jungle country the Americans had little use for artillery and Gatling guns. Over a thousand engagements were fought.

The leader of the rebellion, Emilio Aguinaldo, escaped trap after trap. When General Otis finally weakened Filipino resistance in central Luzon, Aguinaldo and his band hid themselves in the mountain country of northern Luzon. (*See* Map No. 2, page 37.)

The United States Army was bolstered by some of the best officer volunteers in its history, but finding and subduing Aguinaldo seemed a hopeless task. It was like discovering the home base of a will-o'-the-wisp. Finally, through a captive messenger, Colonel Frederick Funston, adventurer and leader from Iola, Kansas, once a helper of Dynamite Johnny O'Brien, learned of Aguinaldo's hiding place. Funston, standing five feet five and not much bigger than Aguinaldo, was fearless. Once, in his youth, because he was interested in the botany of the Arctic, he had paddled alone fifteen hundred miles down the Yukon River.

Funston concocted a plan to capture Aguinaldo and took it to General Arthur MacArthur, who approved. For his combat patrol, Colonel Funston chose eighty-one Filipinos of the Macabebe tribe known to be loyal to the Stars and Stripes. The members of the expedition, except Funston and three other Americans, were disguised as Insurrectos. They steamed away from Manila on a gunboat. At night, about ninety miles from Aguinaldo's secret residence, the colonel and his men went ashore in native canoes. When daybreak filtered through the jungle, the patrol began its march, Funston and the other Americans playing the role of prisoners. The four Americans were surrounded by their "captors."

To deceive the Filipino chieftain, Funston caused a letter signed by one of the Macabebes to be sent ahead, telling Aguinaldo that Funston and a few Americans had been captured and were being brought in as captives.

After five hard days on the trail, the march wound up outside Aguinaldo's bamboo residence. There was a brief fight, and before Aguinaldo knew what was up, he was captured. He accepted the circumstances, and not long afterward he became a respected citizen of the American Philippines. Although his capture ended the insurrection, the burning issue of Philippine independence still remained.

Funston's daring exploit earned him a general's star in the Regular Army. Surprisingly, not every American liked the way Funston captured the Filipino leader. Different generations have different ways of looking at events. Many thought it wrong for an American army officer to use stealth. This feeling almost caused the United States Senate to refuse to confirm Frederick Funston's commission as a brigadier general.

While the soldiers in the Philippines suffered from malaria, attacks of tropical fevers did not strike as hard as they did in Cuba. In the war against Spain and during the time the United States Army was in Cuba—July, 1898, to December, 1900—there were 1,575 cases of yellow fever, with 231 deaths, a mortality rate of about 15 percent.

The disease seemed to travel mysteriously. No one knew for sure how "yellow jack," as the soldiers called it, was transmitted. When a person became ill with yellow jack, others in the vicinity, maybe three houses away, caught it. It seemed almost to travel in the night air. As a result, people in contact with the victims were shunned. No one wanted to shake hands or be close to them. Clothing and bedclothes of the sufferers were handled with sticks and were burned. Walls and floors were washed with disinfectants.

George Sternberg, Surgeon General of the United States Army, decided to make a forceful effort to find out what caused yellow fever. Himself a long-time student of the disease, he had facts on epidemics as far back as 1668. Brigadier General Sternberg, responsible for the health of the army, was appalled by the tragedy in Cuba and by new deaths on the staff of the Governor General in Santiago, Leonard Wood. Sternberg appointed a board of officers to go to Cuba to find out what caused the disease and how to prevent it.

This board, sometimes called the Yellow Fever Commission, had for its president Major Walter Reed. He was the best man Sternberg could find for the job. The general knew that Reed had fourteen years' experience in the army, that he was a skilled pathologist and bacteriologist, unusually quick and observant, who could control people. Reed was forty-nine years old when he landed in Cuba in June, 1900.

On the board with him were Dr. James Carroll, of England, who had served three years in the United States Army and who would handle bacteriological investigations; Dr. Jesse W. Lazear, of Baltimore, Maryland, in charge of mosquito work; and Dr. Aristides Agramonte, of Cuba, who would perform the autopsies and pathological studies. The last two were "acting assistant surgeons" in the army.

Reed reported to Leonard Wood in Havana, and without batting an eye the general approved of Reed's grave but vital request: the use of humans as guinea pigs. The general also made money available. At Quemado de Güines, about 110 miles east of Havana, Reed organized for the job and gave his expert helpers secret instructions. When he asked for volunteers he felt happy because soldiers and civilians— Americans and Spanish—answered his call.

He obtained dozens of mosquitoes, every kind he could lay his hands on. Suddenly a mosquito bit Dr. Carroll, and after a few days he became desperately ill with yellow fever. Fortunately he survived. The excitement in camp rose to a high pitch when Dr. Lazear fell ill with the disease. A month later, on September 25, 1900, Jesse Lazear died.

Reed caused Dr. Lazear's personal effects to be boxed and sent a cablegram to Mrs. Lazear. Reed felt terrible, but with his friend Lazear a martyr to the cause, he pressed ahead.

He now had volunteers sleeping in the foul pajamas of men who had died from the disease, as well as in their very beds. They did this for twenty nights. Nothing happened.

There was a need for a volunteer who would allow himself to be bitten by mosquitoes that had been feeding on patients who had the terrible disease. Private John R. Kissinger, born in Ohio, a hospital steward from the 157th Indiana Volunteer Infantry, stepped forward. Kissinger knew that Walter Reed was almost certain that the disease was transmitted by a mosquito, the *Aëdes aegypti*. The major isolated John Kissinger in a screened room that contained numbers of mongrel mosquitoes. Reed said later, "In my opinion, this exhibition of moral courage has never been surpassed in the Annals of the army of the United States."

Walter Reed's clerk, Mr. John J. Moran, who had been born in Ireland and who had become extremely interested in Reed's experiments, also volunteered to let himself be continually bitten by the deadly mosquitoes. Both Kissinger and Moran refused bonuses which Leonard Wood offered them. Reed said to the two men, "Gentlemen, I salute you."

In a few days yellow fever seized the two volunteers. They became deathly ill, but they did not die because Walter Reed, an expert nurse as well as a smart physician, was able to save them.

With his experiments a success and control of the disease in sight, Reed was delighted. He wrote his wife, "Rejoice with me, sweetheart, ..." and he gave her the details of his successful work.

The news was relayed to the War Department. General Wood published an order from his headquarters in Havana, announcing that it was no longer necessary to wash walls and floors and to take similar precautions against yellow jack, and he told his men why. The order prescribed that oil and kerosene be put in places where mosquitoes could breed.

When the news was published, people all over the earth benefited by the expert and daring work of Walter Reed and his associates. One important dividend was the successful control of yellow fever during the building of the Panama Canal, a work previously abandoned by the French because of their inability to conquer malaria and yellow fever.

In two years Major Reed was dead from appendicitis. Grief was widespread. In his honor the United States Army named its large hospital in Washington, D.C., Walter Reed Army Hospital. People mourned the doctor who seized the opportunity to help mankind by exposing one of the most savage killers of all time.

In 1929 Congress directed the Secretary of War to publish in the official Army Register a "Roll of Honor" giving a description of the part played by each of the twenty-two volunteers. Congress presented a gold medal to each person on the roll or to the representatives of those who had died.

BIBLIOGRAPHY

Alger, R. Alexander, *The Spanish American War*. New York, Harper & Bros., 1901.

American Military History, 1607–1953, Department of the Army. Washington, U.S. Government Printing Office, 1956.

Andrews, Avery DeLano, *My Friend and Classmate John J. Pershing*. Harrisburg, Pennsylvania, The Military Service Publishing Co., 1939.

Army and Navy Journal, March 18, 1899. Washington, D.C.

Azoy, Anastasio M., *Charge!* New York, Longmans, Green & Co., 1961.

Barton, Clara Harlowe, *The Red Cross in Peace and War*. Washington, D.C., American Historical Press, 1899.

Battles and Leaders of the Civil War, Vol. IV. New York, The Century Co., 1888.

Beals, Carleton, *The Crime of Cuba*. Philadelphia, J. B. Lippincott & Co., 1933.

Berryman, John, *Stephen Crane*. New York, Sloane, 1950.

Bigelow, J., *Reminiscences of the Santiago Campaign*. New York, Harper & Bros., 1899.

Boatner, Mark Mayo, III, *The Civil War Dictionary*. New York, David McKay Co., Inc., 1959.

Bocca, Geoffrey, *The Adventurous Life of Winston Churchill.* New York, J. Messner, 1958.

Boykin, Edward, *State of the Union.* New York, Funk & Wagnalls Co., Inc., 1963.

Broad, Lewis, *Winston Churchill, a Biography.* New York, Hawthorn Books, 1963.

Callahan, James Morton, *Cuba and International Relations.* Baltimore, The Johns Hopkins Press, 1899

Canfield, Leon H. and Wilder, Howard B., *The Making of Modern America.* Boston, Houghton Mifflin Co., 1956.

Chadwick, French Ensor, *The Relations of the United States and Spain; The Spanish-American War,* 2 vols. New York, Charles Scribner's Sons, 1911.

Chapman, Charles Edward, *A History of the Cuban Republic.* New York, The Macmillan Co., 1927.

Coblentz, Edmond D., *William Randolph Hearst.* New York, Simon and Schuster, 1952.

Coyle, John G.; McGuire, Edward C.; O'Reilly, Vincent F., *The Journal of the American Irish Historical Society,* Vol. 21. New York, published by the Society, 1922.

Craven, Avery O. and Johnson, Walter, *American History.* New York, Ginn and Co., 1961.

Cullum, George Washington, *Biographical Register of the officers and graduates of the U.S.M.A. at West Point, N.Y.*

Davis, Richard Harding, *Cuba in War Time.* New York, R. H. Russell, 1897.

———— *The Cuban and Porto Rican Campaigns.* New York, Charles Scribner's Sons, 1898.

DeKruif, Paul, *Microbe Hunters.* New York, Harcourt, Brace & Co., 1926.

Dewey, George, *Autobiography.* New York, Charles Scribner's Sons, 1913.

Draper, Andrew S., *The Rescue of Cuba.* Boston, Silver, Burdett & Co., 1899.

Dunn, Harry H., "The man who carried the message to Garcia." American Irish Historical Society Journal, Vol. 21, 1922.

Dunne, Finley Peter, *Mr. Dooley in Peace and in War.* Boston, Small, Maynard & Co., 1899.

Dupuy, R. Ernest and Dupuy, Trevor N., *Military Heritage of America*. New York, McGraw-Hill Book Co., Inc., 1956.

Esposito, Vincent J., Chief Editor, *The West Point Atlas of American Wars*, Vol. 1. New York, Frederick A. Praeger, 1959.

Freidel, Frank, *The Splendid Little War*. Boston, Little, Brown & Co., 1958.

Funston, Frederick, *Memories of Two Wars, Cuban and Philippine Experiences*. New York, Charles Scribner's Sons, 1911.

Ganoe, William Addleman, *The History of the United States Army*. New York, D. Appleton-Century Co., 1942.

Glad, Paul, W., *McKinley, Bryan and the People*. Philadelphia, J. B. Lippincott Co., 1964.

Goode, W. A. M., *With Sampson Through the War*. New York, Doubleday & McClure Co., 1899.

Goodykoontz, Wells, *Major Andrew Summers Rowan*. Washington, Government Printing Office, 1926.

Hagedorn, Hermann, *Leonard Wood*, 2 vols. New York, Harper & Bros., 1931.

Hall, Tom, *The Fun and Fighting of the Rough Riders*. New York, Frederick A. Stokes Co., 1899.

Hancock, Harrie Irving, *What One Man Saw*. New York, Street & Smith, 1900.

Healy, Laurin Hall and Kutner, Luis, *The Admiral*. Chicago, Ziff-Davis Publishing Co., 1944.

Hero Tales of the American Soldier and Sailor ("as told by the heroes themselves and their comrades"). (Place unknown), Hero Publishing Co., 1899.

Hicks, John D., *The American Nation*, Vols. 1 and 2. Boston, Houghton Mifflin Co., 1958.

Hill, Frederic Stanhope, *The Romance of the American Navy*. New York, G. P. Putnam's Sons, 1910.

Hinkel, John V., *Arlington: Monument to Heroes*. Englewood Cliffs, N.J., Prentice-Hall, Inc., 1965.

Hobson, Richmond Pearson, *The Sinking of the "Merrimac."* New York, The Century Co., 1899.

Hohenberg, John, *Foreign Correspondence: The Great Reporters and Their Times*. New York, Columbia University Press, 1964.

Holme, John G., *The Life of Leonard Wood*. New York, Double-day, Page & Co., 1920.

Hubbard, Elbert, *A Message to Garcia and other Essays*. New York, Thomas Y. Crowell, 1924.

Huberman, Leo and Sweezy, Paul M., *Cuba, Anatomy of a Revolution*. New York, Monthly Review Press, 1961.

Jane, Fred T. (editor), *All the World's Fighting Ships*. London, 1901.

Johnson, Gerden F., *History of the Twelfth Infantry Regiment*. Printed privately, 1947.

Jones, Harry W., *A Chaplain's Experience Ashore and Afloat*. New York, A. G. Sherwood & Co., 1901.

Kelly, Howard A., *Walter Reed and Yellow Fever*. Baltimore, The Norman Remington Co., 1906.

Kennan, George, *Campaigning in Cuba*. New York, The Century Co., 1899.

Leech, Margaret, *In the Days of McKinley*. New York, Harper & Brothers, 1959.

Leuchtenburg, William E., "The Needless War with Spain." New York, American Heritage Publishing Co., February 1957 (Vol. VIII, No. 2).

Lodge, Henry Cabot, *The War with Spain*. New York, Harper & Bros., 1899.

Long, John D., *The New American Navy*. New York, The Outlook Co., 1903.

McIntosh, Burr W., *The Little I Saw of Cuba*. New York, F. Tennyson Neely, 1899.

Miley, John D., *In Cuba with Shafter*. New York, Charles Scribner's Sons, 1899.

Millis, Walter, *The Martial Spirit*. Boston, Houghton Mifflin Co., 1931.

Morgan, Howard Wayne, *William McKinley and His America*. Syracuse University Press, 1963.

Morison, Elting E., *The Letters of Theodore Roosevelt*, Vol. II. Cambridge, Massachusetts, 1951. Copyright 1951 by the President and Fellows of Harvard College.

Morison, Samuel Eliot and Commager, Henry S., *The Growth of the American Republic*, Vol. 2. New York, Oxford University Press, 1942.

Mott, Frank Luther, *American Journalism*. New York, The Macmillan Co., 1941.

Navigation Bureau, *Reports of the Navy Department, No. 3, 1898 —Appendix*. Washington, 55th Congress, 3rd Session, 1898–1899.

O'Brien, John, *A Captain Unafraid*. New York, Harper & Bros., 1912.

Olcott, Charles S., *The Life of William McKinley*, 2 vols. Boston, Houghton Mifflin Co., 1916.

Outlook, vol. 91, April 17, 1909. New York, The Outlook Co.

Parker, John Henry, *History of the Gatling Gun Detachment, Fifth Army Corps at Santiago*. Kansas City, Hudson-Kimberly Publishing Co., 1898.

Payne, George Henry, *History of Journalism in the United States*. New York, D. Appleton, 1920.

Post, Charles Johnson, *The Little War of Private Post*. Boston, Little, Brown & Co., 1960.

Pratt, Fletcher, *The Compact History of the United States Navy*. New York, Hawthorn Books, Inc., 1957.

Pringle, Henry F., *Theodore Roosevelt*. New York, Harcourt, Brace & World, Inc., 1956.

Rhodes, Charles D., "William Rufus Shafter." Lansing, Michigan, *Michigan History Magazine*, Vol. XVI (autumn number), 1932.

Robinson, Corinne Roosevelt, *My Brother Theodore Roosevelt*. New York, Charles Scribner's Sons, 1921.

Roosevelt, Theodore, *The Rough Riders*. New York, Charles Scribner's Sons, 1905, 1924.

Rowan, Andrew S., *How I Carried the Message to Garcia*. San Francisco, Walter D. Harney, 1922.

Rowan, Andrew S. and Ramsey, Marathon M., *The Island of Cuba*. New York, Henry Holt & Co., 1896.

Russell, Walter, *Incidents of the Cuban Blockade*. Century Magazine, August 1898.

Sargent, Herbert H., *The Campaign of Santiago de Cuba, (3 vols.)*. Chicago, A. C. McClurg & Co., 1907.

Sargent, Nathan, *Admiral Dewey and the Manila Campaign*. Washington, D.C., Naval Historical Foundation.

Schley, Winfield Scott, *Forty-five Years Under the Flag*. New York, D. Appleton & Co., 1904.

Sexton, William Thaddeus, *Soldiers in the Sun*. Harrisburg, Pennsylvania, The Military Service Publishing Co., 1939.

Smith, O. M. and Wassell, W. H., *History of the Twenty-Second United States Infantry, 1866–1922*. (No other nomenclature.)

Steele, Matthew Forney, *American Campaigns*, 2 vols. Washington, Byron S. Adams, 1909.

Stickney, Joseph L., *With Dewey at Manila*. Harper's New Monthly Magazine, Vol. XCVIII. New York, February 1899.

Swanberg, W. A., *Citizen Hearst*. New York, Charles Scribner's Sons, 1961.

The Life of Admiral Dewey. The Norwich University Record, November, 1937.

Theodore Roosevelt, an Autobiography. New York, Charles Scribner's Sons, 1913, 1923.

Theodore Roosevelt Cyclopedia, Albert B. Hart and Herbert R. Ferleger (editors). New York, Roosevelt Memorial Association, 1941.

The Santiago Campaign; Reminiscences by the Participants. Richmond, Virginia, Williams Printing Co., 1927.

The Spanish American War—Events Described by Eye Witnesses. Chicago, Herbert S. Stone & Co., 1899.

Truby, Albert E., *Memoir of Walter Reed, The Yellow Fever Episode*. New York, Paul B. Hoeber, Inc., Medical Book Dept. of Harper & Bros., 1943.

Vagts, Alfred, *Landing Operations*. Harrisburg, Pennsylvania, Military Service Publishing Co., 1952.

Wallace, Edward S., *Destiny and Glory*. New York, Coward-McCann, Inc., 1957.

Warner, Ezra J., *Generals in Gray*. Louisiana State University Press, 1959.

War Notes 2–5, *Information from Abroad*. Washington, U.S. Office of Naval Intelligence, Government Printing Office, 1899.

Weisberger, Bernard A., *The American Newspaperman*. The University of Chicago Press, 1960–1962.

West, Richard S., Jr., *Admirals of American Empire*. Indianapolis, Bobbs-Merrill Co., 1948.

Wheeler, Joseph, *The Santiago Campaign*. Philadelphia, Drexel Biddle, 1899.

Wilcox, Marrion, *A Short History of the War with Spain*. New York, Frederick A. Stokes Co., 1898.

Wilson, H. W., *The Downfall of Spain—Naval History of the Spanish American War*. London, Sampson, Low, Marston & Co., 1900.

Winkler, John K., *William Randolph Hearst*. New York, Hastings House, 1955.

Young, James Rankin, *History of Our War with Spain*. (Place and publisher unknown) 1898.

Zornow, William F., *Funston Captures Aguinaldo*. New York, American Heritage, February 1958, Vol. IX, No. 2.

INDEX